— THE —
LOVE DRIVEN LIFE

COMPELLED BY THE HIGHEST POWER
TO LIVE THE ULTIMATE LIFE

A. CHRISTIAN

© 2013 Spire Resources, Inc.

Spire Resources, Inc.
PO Box 180
Camarillo, CA 93011
1-800-992-3060
www.spire-resources.com

ISBN 978-1-935843-25-2

Printed in the United States of America

CONTENTS

INTRODUCTION

It's all about love.

That's really what it comes down to.

I already understood that it wasn't about *me*, but I somehow got off track thinking that it was about finding my significance, fulfilling my mission. Like countless other people, I tried desperately to achieve that ideal. I was sincere. I was determined. I was driven.

But I was failing. The harder I tried the more frustrated I felt. I kept pedaling, furiously at times, but my life was like a stationary bike. There was a lot of energy expended, but no progress.

What was I getting wrong?

The answer came, oddly and unexpectedly, in a dream—the most vivid, high-definition, intensely colorful dream I had ever had.

I found myself in a completely unfamiliar place, standing on a meandering dusty path. Nearby, perhaps forty or fifty yards away, were several women at a small stone structure that I somehow knew to be a well. They were busily hoisting large clay jars from the well, water lapping over the sides. I could hear their conversation but the words made no sense to me. One of the women seemed to be telling a story, gesturing in an excited, almost child-like way. She laughed loudly and the others echoed her amusement. They were all dressed like characters in a Bible storybook. But then...so was I.

Even though I was staring at them with such intensity, none of the women seemed to even notice me. I had no urge to approach them. The strangeness of the situation and the foreign cadence of their language made me feel so out of my element. I turned and began to walk down the path, toward no place in particular. I had no idea where I was headed, but I felt compelled to move as if pushed on by some unseen force.

I walked for some distance, perhaps a mile or so. The air was clear, spoiled only by the dust kicked up by my sandals. The path turned sharply to the right, following the natural line of a ridge. I felt the strain in my calf muscles as the climb grew steeper. I kept on hiking, eager to reach the rise that promised downhill relief on the other side. Suddenly, cresting the high point of the path, the robed figure of a man came into view. He was headed directly toward me.

The path was so narrow, it was inevitable that we would meet. But I felt no trepidation. In fact, I felt inexpressible relief.

I began to cry, but had no idea why. With the coarse sleeve of my robe I brushed my tears aside.

His face came into focus—a face more pleasant and inviting than any I had ever seen. As we approached one another, I had many questions on my mind but only one question reached my lips:

"Do you speak English?" I asked.

He smiled warmly and replied, "I speak every language."

I was taken aback by his answer. It just seemed so patently ridiculous. "No one speaks every language," I retorted.

He studied me with a bemused expression and said, "One does."

I challenged him. "Say something to me in some other languages."

He began to rattle off streams of words that, to my untrained ear, did sound like different languages.

"What were you saying?" I quizzed him.

"I was saying the same thing in a dozen different tongues. In your language it will be expressed like this: *For God so loved the world that he gave his one and only Son, that whoever believes in him shall not perish but have eternal life.*"

As soon as the words came out of his mouth he laughed softly.

"What's so funny?" I asked.

"What's funny is that your language doesn't yet exist. Hundreds of years will pass before anyone knows it, speaks it or writes it. But I know it now."

My brain tried to take in what he was claiming. I felt like someone struggling to awake from a stupor. Momentarily seized with anxiety, I blurted out, "Where am I? What year is it?"

"I can't really tell you what year it is. But I can tell you that one day the years themselves will be numbered from the time I spent here on this planet."

"Who are you?" I dared to ask him.

"I am the promised one," he answered firmly.

Then suddenly he said, "I must be on my way."

"Can I go with you?" I asked like a toddler pleading with a parent.

"But you don't know where I'm going," he replied. "And if you did know you would have to think twice about traveling with me."

"Please," I begged him. "Let me walk with you."

"All right," he said, "but I must tell you that the road is not easy."

"I can do it," I assured him, "I'm an experienced hiker."

Again he smiled and replied, "When I said that the road is not easy I wasn't talking about the *actual* road—I was referring to the road *with me*."

I didn't really get it, but I didn't let on to my confusion. "I promise, I won't get in the way."

"I assure you," he said with a tone of finality, "you *will* get in the way; but you'll learn that in time. Just remember to follow me. Let's be on our way."

He stepped past me and started down the path. With the eagerness of a child I followed alongside him. We had walked in silence for perhaps half a mile when he turned to me and said, "What exactly do you want?"

I didn't know what to say. "What do you mean?" I asked.

"Everybody wants something," he said, "but few want the best thing."

Again he asked, "What do you want?"

I was stumped. Was this some sort of trick question? Did he pick up some signal that I wanted something from him?

Was he putting me to a test? I tried to say something but the words were choked off in my parched throat. Nothing came out. I tried again and at last the words broke free: "I guess I want what you were talking about—the best thing. But I don't really know what it is. Maybe that's why I met you. Maybe you're the one to tell me what the best thing is."

His eyes locked with mine. My eyes, I'm sure, were full of confusion. His were full of understanding.

He pivoted to the right and lifted his arm, his outstretched hand pointing to a distant area. "Far to the south," he said, "beyond where we can see, there is a mountain called Sinai. High in that holy place the Prophet Moses received God's Law. In tablets of stone, the finger of God wrote the Commandments that all men are to obey."

"Yes," I said knowingly, "I'm familiar with the Ten Commandments."

"Excellent," he said, "but do you know the Two Commandments?"

Once again I was stumped. "No, I can't say that I do."

"The Ten Commandments—in fact, all of God's Law—rest on Two Commandments. And those Two Commandments have the same core element—Love."

He continued: "If you grasp that truth, you will find what is truly best."

"But how do I do that?" I asked, wanting more than ever to really know.

"Go back to your world," he said, "and search the Scriptures. What you read there will tell you all about me and all about love. I am the subject and love is the theme. You will see that it is true."

"That just seems too simple," I replied.

"Yes," he said, "it is simple. But as I told you before, it is not easy. Read the writings of my servant John. He is a first-hand witness and you can trust everything that he says. He is with me now and hasn't yet written the words you will read, but his testimony is true."

As I processed these instructions, he once again turned and pointed, this time in a different direction. My eye was drawn to the brownish cloth of his robe, hanging loosely from his arm. "Beyond the sea is the land where you will be born. Centuries will pass between now and then, but I will never change. Remember this, and remember that love is supreme." I stared into the distance, thinking hard on his words. I turned to ask him another question but he was gone. Without even the whisper of a sound he had disappeared! I looked for him in all directions, but he had simply vanished. Once again I began to stare into the blurry distance, focused on nothing in particular. I kept telling myself, *Don't forget one word of all that he said. Must not forget...must not forget...must not forget....*

The next thing I heard was the harsh blare of an alarm clock. It seemed out-of-place, modern. I sat up so quickly that I was dazed for a second. As the dizziness passed I began immediately to relive the dream that was unlike any I had ever experienced. The recollections were amazingly clear, and somehow I knew that I had received a message that would influence my life from that point forward.

Later that day I sat down at my desk and began to do what the man in my dream had instructed me to do. "Search the Scriptures," he had said. And, as he had directed, I looked for the subject and the theme. I began by literally looking up that phrase in a Bible concordance (this was before the day of online searches and near-instantaneous results). Discovering that exact phrase— *"Search the Scriptures"*—I felt that I had just found the ticket for a long journey. Many years later, I'm still on the way; my pilgrimage continues. But nothing I have learned so far has ever contradicted what the dream revealed. The man in my dream—whom I believed to be an expression of the God/Man Jesus—has only once again appeared to me in the same way. But that doesn't really bother me because I have learned that he reveals himself in other ways.

Mere hours after my dream, I was "searching the Scriptures" in the Gospel of John, one of the four accounts of the life of Christ. I had started reading in the fifth chapter about an incident in which Jesus was answering some scoffers and doubters. He said to them: *"...The very work that the Father has given me to finish, and which I am doing, testifies that the Father has sent me. And the Father who sent me has himself testified concerning me. You have never heard his voice nor seen his form, nor does his word dwell in you, for you do not believe the one he sent. You diligently study the Scriptures because you think that by them you possess eternal life. These are the Scriptures that testify about me...."*[1]

That final phrase completely arrested my attention: *"These are the Scriptures that testify about me...."* I saw it clearly: The core subject of the Bible is Jesus. It's a book of laws and history and poetry and prophecy; but all of it is organically related to Jesus, the long promised Savior of mankind. I had started reading in chapter five but then went back to the first words of the first chapter:

In the beginning was the Word, and the Word was with God, and the Word was God. He was with God in the beginning. Through him all things were made; without him nothing was made that has been made. In him was life, and that life was the light of men.[2]

The *Word* described in that passage wasn't merely an artifact of grammar. He was—and *is*—the very Source of life and light! As I kept on reading, the ancient text opened to me in a radically new way...

He was in the world, and though the world was made through him, the world did not recognize him. He came to that which was his own, but his own did not receive him. Yet to all who received him, to those who believed in his name, he gave the right to become children of God.[3]

Wow! The One who made this very world chose to enter it in personal form but was not recognized by the majority of people for who he really was. But some did see, some did believe; and to them he gave entrance into God's very family. The idea was overwhelming.

I continued to read John's testimony about the first days of
Jesus' amazing work—how he called the first of his followers,
how he performed his first miracle, how he took a hand-crafted
whip and zealously drove the moneychangers and merchandis-
ers out of God's temple. Then, in the third chapter, I came to
Jesus' encounter with Nicodemus, a prominent member of the
Jewish ruling council. Nicodemus had been impressed with the
itinerant preacher from Galilee: *"Rabbi,"* he said to Jesus, *"we
know you are a teacher who has come from God. For no one could
perform the miraculous signs you are doing if God were not with
him."*[4] In reply, Jesus said, *"I tell you the truth, no one can see
the kingdom of God unless he is born again."*[5]

Apparently confused, Nicodemus asked, *"How can a man
be born when he is old? Surely he cannot enter a second time into
his mother's womb to be born!"* Jesus answered, *"I tell you the
truth, no one can enter the kingdom of God unless he is born of
water and the Spirit. Flesh gives birth to flesh, but the Spirit gives
birth to spirit. You should not be surprised at my saying, 'You
must be born again.' The wind blows wherever it pleases. You hear
its sound, but you cannot tell where it comes from or where it is
going. So it is with everyone born of the Spirit."*[6]

More confounded than ever, Nicodemus asked, *"How can this be?"*[7] I found myself identifying with this guy! He was doing his best to grasp some profound spiritual truths yet Jesus had just reduced the discussion to the seemingly ludicrous idea of being born again. I kept on reading.

> *"You are Israel's teacher," said Jesus, "and do you not understand these things? I tell you the truth, we speak of what we know, and we testify to what we have seen, but still you people do not accept our testimony. I have spoken to you of earthly things and you do not believe; how then will you believe if I speak of heavenly things? No one has ever gone into heaven except the one who came from heaven—the Son of Man. Just as Moses lifted up the snake in the desert, so the Son of Man must be lifted up, that everyone who believes in him may have eternal life."*[8]

I was trying to soak in all these thoughts when I came to the very words that had been spoken in my dream:

> *"For God so loved the world that he gave his one and only Son, that whoever believes in him shall not perish but have eternal life."*[9]

I had first heard these words as a child but this time they affected me in a completely new way. I realized something that I had never really translated to cogent terms. I processed it first as a question: *What drives God?* I had expended so much mental and emotional energy on the question of what drives *me*, but I had never before asked, What drives God? Here in these words I found the answer. *God is driven by love.*

In the words of Jesus himself I realized that the Father was so driven by love for us that he gave his one and only Son to be our Rescuer. The words penetrated deep into my psyche—*For God so loved the world.* I knew it was referring to this world of people, not this physical planet on which we live. He was driven by love for us! He was driven by love for me! I sat there for a moment thinking back to how I have been driven by so many different things in my life—longing for acceptance, desire for wealth, pressure to perform, ambition to succeed. Then it dawned on me: All of those things pale in comparison with what should drive my life. The thought was perfectly framed: I need to be driven by the very thing that drives God himself: *Love.*

I had discovered the key, but now I had to discover the doors that would be opened by that key. Determined to do my best to keep it simple and not mess things up with complications of my own creation, I set out to earnestly explore what it means to live a love-driven life. Along the way, I encountered four overarching truths:

Love is the Mark of the Christian

Love is the Fruit of the Spirit

Love is the Way of the Believer

Love is the Test of the True

These truths have been guideposts for me, repeatedly directing and re-directing my thoughts, actions, reactions and attitudes. These are not mere theoretical concepts; they are transcendent principles, relevant to all of life. Let me state it in very practical terms: Comprehending and then actually living these truths can redeem seemingly hopeless situations, simplify difficult challenges, save failing relationships, bring clarity to confused situations and so much more. I would not have believed this to be possible, but it is. My hope is that you too will experience these things in a deeply personal way as you endeavor to live a love-driven life.

CHAPTER ONE

THE MARK

Love is the Mark of the Christian

"By this all men will know that you are
my disciples, if you love one another."
John 13:35

I first noticed the tattoo when she reached to receive a drink from the flight attendant. It was faded and difficult to make out, but it was definitely a tattoo. My curiosity was aroused. *Why would an elegantly dressed elderly woman have a tattoo on her arm?* I summoned the courage to speak to her.

"Would you mind my asking about the tattoo on your arm?" I inquired almost sheepishly.

She studied my face momentarily with a wry grin then thrust out her left arm for me to see plainly what I had only glimpsed before. The tattoo turned out to be a crudely fashioned and somewhat jumbled string of numbers. Over time, ink that was once black had become a faint blue.

She still had not spoken a word.

"What is it?" I asked, feeling somewhat foolish but even more intrigued.

"*That*," she said with emphasis, "is the mark that defines my life."

The words were delivered in a strong voice, full of conviction. I clearly understood, in spite of her thick Germanic accent.

Her arm still outstretched, we both studied the coarse markings. I for the first time; she for perhaps the millionth. As I stared at the unsightly tattoo she spoke again.

"I was 19 when they did that to me," she said in a dispassionate tone. "By then I had already been separated from my family. I was a star athlete, very healthy and strong. That's why they singled me out for the manual labor."

For the next two hours, as we cruised along at 35,000 feet, she told me her astonishing story of survival through years of imprisonment in the Nazi concentration camp at Auschwitz in southern Poland. A place of unimaginable horrors, Auschwitz was designated by Hitler's Third Reich as the primary site for "the final solution"—the extermination of European Jews. In less than three years, more than three million people died there. Two-and-a-half-million lives were snuffed out in the gas chambers; the other half-million perished from disease and starvation.

At one point in our conversation, after a somber pause, she stated flatly: "Among those millions who died were all the members of my family. I was the only one who survived." She went on to tell me of her bittersweet sense of deliverance when the camp was liberated in the winter of 1945. She was alive, but what lay ahead? Alone and penniless, what would her future be?

I was pleased to learn that after the war she met and married a young American officer. Together they built a new life and a family of their own. But she told me frankly, "Not a day passes that I don't relive something of those years in the camp." I thought back to her first words to me: "*That* is the mark that defines my life."

It wasn't merely a tattoo. It was the symbol of unforgettable sadness, tragedy, deprivation and suffering. Ultimately, there was freedom for her; but it was a hollow freedom in many ways, bereft of the ones to whom she was closest. She told me how difficult it had been to live without fear even after the reasons to fear were long past. Holding on to the promise of good things to come was, she admitted, a never-ending challenge.

I have often recalled that woman's captivating story, and

each time I have been drawn back to her first words: "*That is the mark that defines my life.*" Her statement has prompted me to ask myself: *What is the mark that defines my life?* I don't have a tattoo on my arm or any other part of my body that stands as a literal symbol of my identity and my experience. But surely there is a mark that should define my life.

In fact, Jesus described such a mark. On the night that he was villainously betrayed, Jesus was gathered with his disciples when he announced unexpectedly: *"My children, I will be with you only a little longer. You will look for me, and just as I told the Jews, so I tell you now: Where I am going, you cannot come."*[1] It was stunning news; and as the weight of his words began to sink in, Jesus added, *"A new command I give you: Love one another. As I have loved you, so you must love one another. By this all men will know that you are my disciples, if you love one another."*[2]

Renowned philosopher Francis Schaeffer wrote, "Through the centuries, men have displayed many different symbols to show that they are Christians. They have worn marks in the lapels of their coats, hung chains about their necks, even had special haircuts. Of course, there is nothing wrong with any of this, if one feels it is his calling. But there is a much better sign—a mark that has not been thought up just as a matter of expediency for use on some special occasion or in some specific era. It is a universal mark that is to last through all the ages of the church till Jesus returns." Schaeffer then concludes, "...It is possible to be a Christian without showing the mark, but if we expect non-Christians to know that we are Christians, we must show the mark."[3]

The mark to which Schaeffer refers—the mark of authentic Christianity—is encapsulated in one word: Love. A short time after Jesus gave his disciples the "new commandment" to love one another, he said this to them: *"As the Father has loved me, so have I loved you. Now remain in my love. If you obey my commands, you will remain in my love, just as I have obeyed my Father's commands and remain in his love. I have told you this so that my joy may be in you and that your joy may be complete. My command is this: Love each other as I have loved you. Greater love has no one than this, that he lay down his life for his friends."*[4] Then Jesus repeated the earlier admonition: *"This is my command: Love each other."*[5]

This instruction shouldn't have come as any surprise to the ragtag group of men who had followed Jesus for three years. They had heard the Master speak on this subject on other occasions. In one incident, two rival groups—the Sadducees and the Pharisees—confronted Jesus. Chapter 22 of Matthew's Gospel gives us a point-for-point account of the interchange. Verse 34 of that passage begins, *Hearing that Jesus had silenced the Sadducees, the Pharisees got together…*[6] Now, before we go any further, let's understand who these two groups are.

The Sadducees were a mostly upper-class sect of Jews who were steeped in religious tradition yet rejected any belief in an afterlife or a resurrection. They were influential and politically engaged. In the Sanhedrin, the 70-member council that governed Jewish life, the Sadducees held the majority of seats and were accommodating to the Romans who ruled the entire region.

The Pharisees, archrivals of the Sadducees, were fervent rule keepers—not just the biblical rules but hundreds of other regulations that had been added to and pronounced as equal to Scripture. Unlike the Sadducees, the Pharisees believed in a coming resurrection of the dead and an afterlife determined by divine judgment and reward. The groups were united in one thing however: their hatred of Jesus. For very different reasons, they both considered him a formidable threat.

Now, back to verse 34: *Hearing that Jesus had silenced the Sadducees, the Pharisees got together.* And why did the Pharisees get together? To succeed where the Sadducees had failed. They had their own experts ready to ask an even better trick question, one sure to entrap this rabbi named Jesus who was gaining quite a following and stirring up an uncomfortable level of interest.

In a previous confrontation, the Pharisees had already tried to paint Jesus into a corner. Their first attempt didn't pan out, but they were not about to surrender. The group-think of the Pharisees seems to be, "Okay, our first guy couldn't trip him up; the Sadducees couldn't handle it; but we can't just leave this alone. We'll have one of our really, really smart guys ask him the ultimate trick question. Jesus will fail the test and be revealed for the phony that he is." Or so they thought. Matthew describes what happened next:

> *One of them, an expert in the law, tested him with this question: "Teacher, which is the greatest commandment in the Law?"*[7]

On the surface, the question seems honest enough, but the intent was far from honest. The questioner is "an expert in the law." This description identifies him as a Pharisee who had memorized the entire Torah, the first five books of the Old Testament—Genesis, Exodus, Leviticus, Numbers and Deuteronomy. He knew it all, word for word! It's hard enough for us to read a book like Leviticus, much less memorize it! He is an expert. He knows.

Keep in mind that for the Pharisees keeping rules was paramount. They had painstakingly identified and numbered 613 commandments—248 positive, 365 negative. All 613 (including the Ten Commandments) had been divided into two categories: *heavy* laws and *light* laws. The Pharisees taught that if you violated one of the *heavy* laws you were in big trouble—a God's-going-to-get-you type of trouble. But if you violated one of the *light* laws, then please just apologize and try not to make that same mistake again. They constantly debated all these rules and regulations among themselves and with the Sadducees and Herodians (another Jewish sect). They would make competing cases for which of the *heavy* laws was the most important, the most significant. But it was commonly believed among them that there was no provable right answer to the question, *Which is the greatest commandment in the Law?*

We can almost imagine the Pharisees discussing their

strategy with all the earnestness of a high school debate team. "What's the one question that Jesus couldn't possibly answer? Let's nail him with that one!" But Jesus had a surprising reply. Not only did he answer the which-is-the-greatest question, he also answered which is the second greatest:

> *"Jesus replied: 'Love the Lord your God with all*
> *your heart and with all your soul and with all*
> *your mind.' This is the first and greatest com-*
> *mandment. And the second is like it: 'Love your*
> *neighbor as yourself.' All the Law and the*
> *Prophets hang on these two commandments."* [8]

Without hesitating, without flinching, Jesus answered the "expert's" question. He did so by quoting from Deuteronomy chapter 6, traditionally the first passage of Scripture that any Jewish boy or girl learned in life. It begins, *Hear, O Israel: The Lord our God, the Lord is one. Love the Lord your God with all your heart and with all your soul and with all your strength.*[9] Jesus says categorically, *"This is the first and greatest commandment."* He doesn't wobble around; he doesn't struggle for words. He says flatly, this is #1. Then he adds a statement from Leviticus 19, *"Love your neighbor as yourself."*[10] We have to wonder if they're thinking, 'Wait!

We didn't ask you for the second greatest!' Then Jesus delivers the punch line:

> *"All the Law and the Prophets hang on these two commandments."*[11]

With a few simple words Jesus upsets everything in their system. They have a veritable catalog of laws, some biblical and some of their own invention. They've been debating for centuries about the relative value of all these rules and regulations. They've piled hundreds of interpretive codes on top of the laws themselves. Jesus suddenly makes it so simple by quoting one verse from Deuteronomy and another from Leviticus. He tells them, *"Love the Lord your God with all your heart and with all your soul and with all your mind...Love your neighbor as yourself."*

The energy that moves us spiritually and relationally does not come from being right, being superior, or being compliant with a list of rules and regulations. It comes from *love*, not from law. The mark of the true Christian is authentic love for God and for other people. Our emotions don't produce this kind of love. Nor can we generate this love by sheer will power. We are energized to love only by staying connected to the power source of God's love. We maintain that connection by our obedience to him. Think back to what Jesus told his disciples on the night he was betrayed: *"As the Father has loved me, so have I loved you. Now remain in my love. If you obey my commands, you will remain in my love, just as I have obeyed my Father's commands and remain in his love."*[12] We remain in God's love when we remain obedient to him, and that very obedience keeps us plugged into his limitless power. The result is a life of total fulfillment. As Jesus said, *"I have told you this so that my joy may be in you and that your joy may be complete."*[13]

In an incident similar to the one described in Matthew 22, the Gospel of Luke tells about another "expert" in Old Testament Law who attempted to test Jesus. Luke says that he stood up and asked, *"Teacher, what must I do to inherit eternal life?"*[14] Jesus replied, *"What is written in the Law? How do you read it?"*[15] The man answered: *"'Love the Lord your God with all your heart and with all your soul and with all your strength and with all your mind'; and, 'Love your neighbor as yourself.'"*[16] Jesus then said, *"You have answered correctly. "Do this and you will live."*[17] Not satisfied with the answer, he asked Jesus, *"And who is my neighbor?"*[18] In reply, Jesus told one of the most memorable stories in history, the Parable of the Good Samaritan:

"A man was going down from Jerusalem to Jericho, when he fell into the hands of robbers. They stripped him of his clothes, beat him and went away, leaving him half dead. A priest happened to be going down the same road, and when he saw the man, he passed by on the other side. So too, a Levite, when he came to the place and saw him, passed by on the other side. But a Samaritan, as he traveled, came where the man was; and when he saw him, he took pity on him. He went to him and bandaged his wounds, pouring on oil and wine. Then he put the man on his own donkey, took him to an inn and took care of him. The next day he took out two silver coins and gave them to the innkeeper. 'Look after him,' he said, 'and when I return, I will reimburse you for any extra expense you may have.'"[19]

Jesus then asked the questioner: *"Which of these three do you think was a neighbor to the man who fell into the hands of robbers?"*[20] The lawyer replied, *"The one who had mercy on him."*[21] Jesus said in response, *"Go and do likewise."*[22]

The man was correct in identifying the two great commandments: To love God with all your heart and with all your soul and with all your strength and with all your mind, and to love your neighbor as yourself. In telling the parable of the Good Samaritan, Jesus illustrated the second part of that equation: *How* to love your neighbor as yourself. The story itself is a captivatingly beautiful portrait of love-driven behavior. The Samaritan's life was marked by love; and that love was expressed in all of his actions, reactions and attitudes. Let's take a closer look and learn from his example....

Love drives us to see people as God sees them.

Robbers on the rugged, often-treacherous road between Jerusalem and Jericho had viciously attacked a man. They stripped him of his clothes; beat him mercilessly; stole everything he had; then tossed him to the side of road, leaving him half-dead. Two so-called religious men—a priest and a Levite (an assistant in the Temple)—walked by the scene of the crime, saw the man lying there bloody and battered and deliberately chose to ignore him. In fact, they avoided even getting close to him by crossing over to the other side of the road! Then along came the Samaritan. The very fact that he was on that road in that place put him at a severe disadvantage. He was in Jewish territory, well beyond his home turf of Samaria, many miles to the north. He was traveling a path known to be dangerous. He was also a despised outsider, for Jews had nothing to do with Samaritans.[23] Like the priest and the Levite, the Samaritan saw the injured man; unlike them, he saw with eyes of love that perceived suffering and pain. Others were able to callously ignore what they had seen and keep on trekking down the road. Not the Samaritan.

When we are driven by love we are able to look at people and see the reality of their needs, the frailty of their situation and the consequences if they are ignored. One who bears the mark of the Christian—authentic love—looks at others and sees them as fellow human beings made in the image of God. Real love looks at others without regard to their race, their religion, their social status, their political persuasions, their wealth or poverty, their outward beauty or ugliness. Love sees every other person as a "neighbor" worthy of love. Paul wrote to the Christians at Rome: *Let no debt remain outstanding, except the continuing debt to love one another.*[24] We *owe* others our love.

Love drives us to suffer with those who suffer.

When he looked at the stranger on the side of the road, bloody and beaten and helpless, the Samaritan reacted with compassion. He felt the man's pain. He dared to suffer the man's suffering. It wasn't enough to see him; he had to actually feel for him. This is the essence of compassion: to feel another person's pain. The word *compassion* literally means *to suffer another's suffering*. This is completely contrary to our natural human inclinations; we don't by nature opt for pain. When faced with the choice between difficulty and ease, we are drawn to the easy alternative. But the reality is that life slams us with hard things: loss, disease, grief, heartache, struggle. When we go through those tough experiences we need more deeply than we can imagine the compassion of others who are willing to truly feel our pain. On the other hand, when we see others going through those life-slamming times, love drives us to willingly suffer with those who suffer.

Love drives us to act even when it's inconvenient.

The Samaritan saw the injured man, felt deep compassion for him and was driven by love to take action. His compassion translated into determined, decisive acts. He stepped off the path and went to the man. It wasn't convenient (and may not have been safe); but love prompts us to act even when it's inconvenient. Throughout life we will often be confronted with the problems of other people, and it seldom (perhaps never) comes at a convenient time. This is an inevitable reality. It may be a best friend who comes to you sobbing with the news of a spouse's infidelity. It may be the latest crisis for the prickly relative whose life seems to be overshadowed with a permanently fixed dark cloud. Maybe it's a co-worker who just got the devastating news of a cancer diagnosis. Or perhaps it's the homeless stranger who sits on the curbside holding a crudely fashioned cardboard sign, silently begging for something, anything.

Love is not concerned with convenience. It stands willing to be bothered, ready to be interrupted. It takes time to listen to bad news without any regard or interest in later spreading that news as gossip. It patiently endures the irritation of an unpleasant personality. It weeps with the one who weeps. It reaches out to the one who is confused, hungry, in pain. It discerns that confusion; it identifies with that hunger; it senses that pain. But it doesn't just feel. Love is driven to act.

**Love drives us to get involved
when others don't (or won't).**

The Samaritan was driven by love to intervene. He was not afraid to stoop down to help, to get his hands dirty with the blood and grit of a stranger's wounds. Love stirs us to get involved when others don't (or won't).

A friend of mine served for several years as a teacher in a Latin American nation that was wracked at the time by a brutal civil war. He could have returned to the relative safety of the U.S., but chose to stay in that troubled place and finish his term. When he'd accepted the assignment, there was apparent peace and stability in the land. That changed dramatically within a few months after he arrived. It had never occurred to him that he would find himself living and working in a desperately dangerous place. When the troubles began as a series of seemingly random kidnappings, he was alarmed but not yet fearful. Then as the violence escalated into clashes between rival factions and bombings on a near-daily basis he had to re-think why he was there and whether he should stay. As a Christian, he felt that God had opened the doors to this opportunity to teach; and though he prayed at times for God's permission to leave, the answer was an overwhelming spiritual sense to stay.

One night as he arrived to teach a class for adults he saw one of his students sitting on the steps of the institute, his head buried in his hands. He walked up to him and reached down to touch his shoulder. "Roberto*," my friend said to him, "what's the matter? Has something happened?" The student looked up and a gush of tearful words poured out of him. Sobbing at times uncontrollably, he explained that he had just gotten word that his brother had been killed near the campus of the national university. He had been in the wrong place at the wrong time, the victim of gunfire from a skirmish in which he had no part. Roberto said that the responsibility fell on him to retrieve the body and bury his brother, but that the family had no money and no one to whom they could turn for help.

My friend knew in that instant at least one of the reasons why God had not given him permission to leave. He pulled Roberto to his feet and said, "Let's go take care of your brother." Leaving instructions for the teaching assistant to take care of the class, they headed for the city morgue. Some fifteen minutes later they arrived and began to make inquiries. After a brief wait they were directed to a macabre, dimly lit room where corpses in various states lay on gray stone slab tables. Though shocked by the sight, they held emotions in check and began to search the room, finally locating the body of Roberto's brother. He was so disfigured and bloody that Roberto recognized him only by his clothing. My friend turned to his visibly shaken student and said, "We're going to need some new clothes for him, Roberto." He reached into his pocket and took out some cash. "Here, take this," he said. "Go and buy something that will fit him and I'll take care of things here until you get back." Reluctant at first, Roberto left to buy an outfit for his dead loved one.

My friend then began what he describes as the most unpleasant but necessary thing he has ever done: removing the blood-drenched clothing and cleaning the body of a complete stranger. After doing the best he could, he covered the body with a greenish sheet he found on a nearby shelf. When Roberto returned they worked together to dress the body, signed some forms, and then carried the lifeless form to my friend's VW bus and gently laid him in the back section (which was seatless at the time). Next, they drove to a funeral parlor to purchase a simple casket. After carefully placing the body in the plain wooden box, they drove to Roberto's home in an impoverished area that bordered a slum. They unloaded the casket and carried it in, gingerly making their way through a small crowd of family members and neighbors who had gathered. It was the beginning of a grieving process that would go on until the burial service the next morning.

After a few somber words with several family members, my friend quietly made his way back to his car. "As I drove back home," he later said, "I thought about the Good Samaritan. I realized that if I hadn't intervened, chances are no one else would have. I think I was the only one who could have helped. God put me there in that moment, and God gave me the strength to get involved. Few experiences in life are as dramatic and as wrenching as that, but the one thing I took away from it is that I have to always be ready to respond in love regardless of the exact circumstances or conditions. I think that's what God intends for us."

Like the Samaritan, my friend was driven by love to help, giving no thought to himself. He chose not to "mind his own business." The care in his heart was matched by the care of his hands. His experience answers the question that John raised in his first epistle: *If anyone has material possessions and sees his brother in need but has no pity on him, how can the love of God be in him?*[25] Again, it comes back to that: The life of real meaning and lasting impact is the life that is driven by love.

Love drives us to give sacrificially and willingly.

The Samaritan was driven by love to give. Sacrificially and willingly, he gave everything at his disposal—bandages (perhaps pieces of his own clothing?), oil and wine (expensive commodities in that era), and his own donkey to transport his "patient" to a nearby inn. In choosing comfort for the stranger, he chose discomfort for himself. With extraordinary generosity he even paid for the stranger's lodging at the inn.

Love always comes at a cost because it is always directed outward, not inward; and it demands that we pay a price in time, energy and the resources at hand. The price may be high—in fact, it may be extreme. As Jesus told his disciples, *"Greater love has no one than this, that he lay down his life for his friends."*[26] Of course, that is precisely what Jesus did. He laid down his life for his friends; and to all who believe and receive him he offers the gift of his very life, eternal life. His love-driven sacrifice—greater than any other ever made—paid the ultimate of all prices.

Love drives us to commit above and beyond.

The Samaritan was driven by love to commit. He stayed engaged and literally went the extra mile on behalf of a stranger who offered nothing to him in return. After reaching the inn, he kept on caring, giving even more of his time in tending to the wounded one. Upon leaving the inn to continue on his journey he gave an additional sum of money for the lodging and care of the recovering man, then made a further commitment to pay even more upon his return to the inn.

True love is willing and ready to commit. It says to another person, *I'm going to give to you and I'm not going to give up on you.* This is absolutely essential to a healthy marriage relationship, of course; but it applies equally to other relationships in which God gives us the opportunity to demonstrate his love through our actions, reactions and attitudes. Driven purely by his love for us, God willingly committed his one and only Son to rescue and redeem us. And driven purely by love, he keeps his promise to care for us. As a compassionate Father he longs for the best in his children. His desire is that we bear the mark of our relationship to him, just as a child bears the features of a parent. The highest and best semblance, of course, is the mark of authentic love. When we show that mark—by loving him and by loving others—we reveal to a watching world that we are exactly who we claim to be.

CHAPTER TWO
THE FRUIT
LOVE IS THE FRUIT OF THE SPIRIT

The fruit of the Spirit is love...
Galatians 5:22

Thomas first noticed the children as he prepared to board a train at New Delhi's main depot. Huddled together under a flimsy blanket, they stared straight ahead, the frayed cloth pulled up to their chins. There seemed to be not a hint of emotion in their faces, but Thomas sensed fear in their eyes. The platform was teeming as always with thousands of travelers, a mass of noisy humanity. His train was departing momentarily, but Thomas walked over to the three children. He knelt down and spoke to the oldest, a boy perhaps nine or ten years old.

"What's your name, son? he asked.

"My name is Rajeev**, sir," said the boy in quick reply.

"Do you belong to someone?" Thomas inquired. In a nation with literally millions of orphaned and abandoned children it was a perfectly legitimate question.

"We're waiting on our father," the boy answered nervously. The youngster forced a smile.

Thomas smiled in return and said, "I hope he comes for you soon." He stood to his feet, looked down once again at the ragged children, then made his way to the Second Class railcar. The final all-aboard whistle sounded as he stepped onto the train.

The next day, Thomas returned to New Delhi, arriving at the same platform. As he departed the train he caught sight of the same children, still huddled in the very same place. It was as if they had not moved a muscle in over 24 hours. More than a bit curious, he strode directly to them, once again kneeling down to speak to them at eye-level.

"So your father hasn't yet arrived?" he asked.

The older boy shook his head and said, "No sir, he hasn't come back."

Thomas's brow furrowed with concern. "When did he leave you here?"

The boy looked downward as he replied, "Four days ago. My brother and sister and I have been right here since he left us. He said, 'stay right there. I'll be back for you soon.' But we still wait."

Thomas knew that the father would not be coming back.

"Where is your mother?" he asked.

The boy answered with sad matter-of-factness, "She died last year."

Looking at each of the children one by one, Thomas knew that they had nothing and no one. They were utterly alone.

"Tonight you will eat a good meal and sleep in a warm bed. You will come with me to a place that is unlike any place you have ever been in your life. We will ride on the train for about three hours and then we will be there." He extended his hand to the youngest, a girl of four or five. She grasped his thumb and Thomas helped her to her feet. Without hesitation, all three children tagged along with the kindly man whose face was surely the happiest they had ever seen. He bought their tickets and the party of four boarded the train to Kota, a city of nearly two million souls.

Arriving at the Kota depot, Thomas was greeted by half a dozen young men and women, staff members from the Emmanuel Children's Home—an amazing place filled with love and joy and over 1,500 contented boys and girls. Rajeev and his little brother and sister would soon join them. That night they would experience the satisfaction of a full stomach and the comfort of a cozy bed—just as the man had promised. Soon they would have new clothes, new friends and a school where they would be taught everything they longed to learn. It would be their first night in the place they would call home for many years to come. Rajeev and his siblings had been rescued by M. A. Thomas, an extraordinary man described in one news report as "the one who loves the unloved."

When he graduated from college in Madras in 1960, M. A. Thomas had only 200 rupees to his name—the equivalent of just $8—and virtually no earthly possessions. But his heart held an inexpressibly great treasure that he was eager to share—a profound desire to help everyone that God would enable him to help. With his wife, Ammini, then pregnant with their first child, M. A. was determined to head for the Indian state of Rajasthan—considered at the time the most spiritually challenging and needy place in all of India. The young couple was prepared to walk the 1,000 miles to this place they had never seen, without the promise of a job or a place to stay.

A few days before they were to set out on their journey, M.A. and Ammini met a distinguished visitor from the U.S., a man named Bill Bright. Dr. Bright, founder of the worldwide Christian ministry now known as Cru, listened to M.A.'s testimony and was impressed with the young man's remarkable determination. He took $25 from his pocket and gave it to M.A., with the promise that he would continue to send at least that much every month in missionary support (a promise Bill Bright kept for over 40 years).

Using a portion of the $25 gift, M.A. purchased train tickets to Kota, Rajasthan, still with no idea what lay ahead. Arriving in Kota on a blistering day in August, M.A. went to the most prominent intersection and began to preach the Gospel. He was promptly arrested, jailed, beaten and ordered by the magistrate to leave the city. After his release, he went back to the same intersection and began to preach the same message! Again, he was arrested; but his joyous attitude confounded the authorities.

"Why are you here? And why won't you leave?" the judge demanded to know.

He replied, "I'm here to tell the Good News to every person I can, and I can't leave because God sent me here."

The judge was intrigued. "What is this 'good news' you have?" he asked. So M.A. shared Christ's message of hope and salvation with him.

The judge was curious, but first he wanted to know why anyone would be interested in the poor.

"Because Jesus loved the poor and the outcasts, I love them, too," M.A. answered. In a culture where cows are valued more highly than some human beings, it was a radical thing to say. Reluctantly, the judge jailed the bold young preacher for the night; but he rescinded the order that he leave the city.

Over the next 50 years M.A. Thomas became the most beloved man in Kota. In fact, he became a beloved figure in every region of India and was honored with the Padma Shri, one of the nation's highest civilian awards. He never stopped preaching the Good News or daring to touch the "untouchables" of society. Over his half-century of ministry, M.A. dealt with countless crises and challenges; but along the way he founded a college, trained thousands of ministers, built a hospital, started numerous clinics, created a network of schools and established nearly a hundred children's homes across the length and breadth of India. The largest of those homes, the Emmanuel Children's Home in Kota, was the first orphanage he established. Today it is a community of hundreds of boys and girls like Rajeev and his siblings who otherwise wouldn't know the security of a safe home, the satisfaction of a good meal or the joy of a loving embrace. But they know all that and more because years ago one man decided to live a radically counter-cultural, love-driven life.

I interviewed M. A. Thomas numerous times both in the U.S. and in his native India. I also heard him speak to large audiences, each time marveling at his ability to simultaneously engage people of widely varied backgrounds. In one of our far-ranging conversations, we were discussing the array of challenges he faced daily in India—indescribably deep poverty, religious persecution, the blight of leprosy, countless orphaned and abandoned children, widows without hope, innumerable blind, deaf and lame left to fend for themselves.

I asked, "How do you decide where and when to help? There are so many problems faced by so many people—how do you even know where to begin?"

M. A. gestured with upraised palms and said, "You begin with the person right in front of you, with the need staring you in the face. You recognize that you are on a path, and on that path you will meet many people who need your help and you will see many things that cry for your intervention. At every point, with every person and with every situation, you must ask, *'How would Jesus love this person? How would he express the Father's concern?'"*

I saw in M.A.'s life the fruit of his consistent, positive responses to that question: children rescued from deprivation; lepers whose sores were being tenderly treated; widows with a renewed sense of worth; villages blessed by Christ-centered ministry—many of them receiving the Gospel for the first time ever. I said to M.A., "There are so many believers who struggle to live a fruitful life. They look at someone like you and wonder how they can ever experience the kind of significance that you have." M.A. replied, "I think it always comes down to love itself, because love is the fruit of the Spirit."

He reached across a desk stacked high with papers to retrieve a well-worn Bible from a wooden book trough. He opened it to Paul's epistle to the Galatians, chapter five. He began to read at verse 22... *But the fruit of the Spirit is love, joy, peace, patience, kindness, goodness, faithfulness, gentleness and self-control.*[1] The Bible still open in his hand, he turned to me and said, "I used to look at this as a list of desirable qualities that are fruits of a Spirit-controlled life; but I've come to believe that the fruit itself is love, and all the other virtues are part and parcel of that one fruit. The original

Greek word is singular, not plural. It is *fruit*, not *fruits*. I think this is significant, and to me it indicates that all the other things that Paul lists are by-products of love. You can't have joy without love. You can't have peace without love. You can't be patient without love. You can't have any of these other qualities apart from love."

He paused for a few seconds then continued, "I think this reflects what Jesus taught about love being the summation of God's law. You can see that Paul had that same understanding. He starts this passage with a key statement in verse 13: *You, my brothers, were called to be free. But do not use your freedom to indulge the sinful nature; rather, serve one another in love. The entire law is summed up in a single command: Love your neighbor as yourself.*[2] By 'entire law' he's talking about the entire law that governs human relationships. The command is very clear: Love your neighbor as yourself. But of course, you can only do that if your life is controlled by God's Spirit. He empowers us to live a life of love."

After my conversation with M. A. I began to search the Scriptures for connections between love and those eight qualities listed in Galatians 5:22-23. I was in for some rich discoveries as I examined each virtue one by one. The first thing I learned is that a love-driven life is...

A Life Filled with Joy

Check virtually any thesaurus and you'll find a long list of synonyms for joy. Some of the most frequently-used examples include: amusement, bliss, cheer, delight, diversion, ecstasy, elation, gladness, glee, gratification, happiness, hilarity, humor, jubilance, liveliness, merriment, pleasure, rapture, refreshment, satisfaction, wonder. And there are many more! But these words reveal only certain qualities of joy, much like a brilliant light reflects only certain facets of a gemstone. None of these terms captures the full meaning of joy in the biblical sense of the word. That's because the joy referred to in Scripture is transcendent. It is beyond understanding, beyond complete description.

There's a big distinction, for example, between happiness and joy. Happiness is almost always dependent upon favorable circumstances or conditions. We are happy when things are going well and life is in sync. We are unhappy when things are not going our way and when life (or even a small part of it) is jumbled or messy. Joy, on the other hand, is not subject to circumstances or conditions. Even in the throes of the most severe difficulties it is possible to be joyful. In fact, as followers of Jesus, we are supposed to be joyful in tough times. James the Apostle wrote, *Consider it pure joy, my brothers, whenever you face trials of many kinds, because you know that the testing of your faith develops perseverance.*[3]

Jesus taught that joy springs from love. He said to his disciples, *"As the Father has loved me, so have I loved you. Now remain in my love. If you obey my commands, you will remain in my love, just as I have obeyed my Father's commands and remain in his love. I have told you this so that my joy may be in you and that your joy may be complete."*[4] Inspired by their Master, the disciples were driven by love to obey him regardless of the circumstances. As a result, the joy of Jesus himself would totally fill their hearts. Their lives would bear the fruit of the Spirit, love; and that perfect love would yield perfect joy. The road ahead of them would not be easy. Quite to the contrary: it would be rugged and dangerous. Consider how their earthly journeys came to an end...

> JAMES ZEBEDEE, the first of the faithful apostles to die, was beheaded by edict of King Herod.

SIMON PETER was crucified by order of the wicked emperor Nero. At his own request, Peter was crucified head down in a final expression of honor to the Lord Jesus.

ANDREW was lashed with a whip then tied to an X-shaped cross where he hung for two days before dying.

PHILIP was crucified.

BARTHOLOMEW was beaten, flayed, then crucified head down.

THOMAS was speared by idolatrous priests then burned in an oven.

MATTHEW was axed to death.

JAMES ALPHAEUS was thrown from the Temple tower but did not die; in fierce anger his oppressors then clubbed him to death.

THADDAEUS was crucified.

SIMON THE ZEALOT was crucified.

MATTHIAS, the Apostle chosen to replace Judas, was stoned and beheaded.

JOHN, son of Zebedee and brother of James, was thrown into boiling oil but miraculously suffered no injuries. He died of natural causes and was buried near Ephesus about 100 AD— making him the only one of the Apostles not to die a violent death.

According to patristic writings from the early centuries of the Church, many of the Apostles voiced loud prayers of rejoicing, sang praises and even laughed as their earthly lives ended! Their joyful willingness to die for Christ confounded their persecutors. But as faithful "followers of the Way" they were doing exactly what their Lord had done. Jesus was brutally beaten, callously ridiculed, nailed to a roughly hewn cross, and cruelly hoisted up to die in excruciating pain beside two common thieves. The Apostles had seen it all. They were eyewitnesses of their Master's inexpressibly great love, and when their time for suffering was at hand they faced it in exactly the same way—with joyous love. Perhaps the author of the epistle to the Hebrews had them in mind when he wrote, *Therefore, since we have so great a cloud of witnesses surrounding us, let us also lay aside every encumbrance and the sin which so easily entangles us, and let us run with endurance the race that is set before us, fixing our eyes on Jesus, the author and perfecter of faith, who for the joy set before Him endured the cross, despising the shame, and has sat down at the right hand of the throne of God.*[5]

What was *"the joy set before him"* that moved Jesus to endure such suffering and pain, to literally give himself as a sacrifice for us? It was the joy of reunion with the Father, the joy of re-entering the glories of heaven he had left behind when he *"made himself nothing"*[6] and became human. It was the joy of finishing his mission to seek and save the lost. It was the joy of bringing perfect glory to the Father. Jesus—our love-driven Savior—kept sight of the joy set before him and did what he alone could do.

What about us? What is the joy set before us that compels us to live with true significance? It is the same joy on which Jesus focused all his emotions and energies. The ultimate reward of a love-driven, joy-filled life is union with the Father and the wonder of eternity with him. Only by setting our hearts on the life to come can we experience true joy in life here and now. Paul counseled the Colossian believers, *Set your minds on things above, not on earthly things.*[7] Then he told them how: *As God's chosen people, holy and dearly loved, clothe yourselves with compassion, kindness, humility, gentleness and patience. Bear with each other and forgive whatever grievances you may have against one another. Forgive as the Lord forgave you.*[8] Then he adds the key: *And over all these virtues put on love, which binds them all together in perfect unity.*[9] In other words, love is the glue that holds everything together. Its fruit in our lives will be revealed in confoundingly great joy that transcends all the tough times and endures in the face of the most unfavorable circumstances and conditions.

A Life Ruled by Peace

The very next statement in Paul's letter to the Colossians is timeless advice to believers: *Let the peace of Christ rule in your hearts, since as members of one body you were called to peace.*[10] The operative word in Paul's statement is *rule*. It is the same Greek root from which we get the word *umpire*. The Apostle is saying, in effect, *Let the peace of Christ be the umpire in your hearts*. This is an easy concept for us to grasp. Envision an umpire in a baseball game—calling balls and strikes, declaring runners safe or out, breaking up scuffles, making all sorts of near-instantaneous judgments. The role of the umpire is to maintain order and keep the game on an even keel. And so it is with the role of peace in our hearts. It is the umpire that facilitates wise decisions and ensures mental and emotional balance.

Peace, in the biblical sense of the word, is like Joy: it defies measurement. Paul wrote to the Philippians: *...the peace of God, which transcends all understanding, will guard your hearts and your minds in Christ Jesus.*[11] God's peace surpasses human comprehension; it exceeds anything we can fully grasp. I find this reassuring because my tendency is to do everything possible to stay in control, to be my own umpire. But if I'm in control, God is not. If the peace I have in my mind and heart is manufactured by my own scheming, then it's not a real peace. It is only when I am driven by love that I am ruled by peace.

In this troubled, tormented world there are wars and rumors of wars without end. There is strife, crime and corruption at every level of society, in every place on earth. There is so much bad news and so much cause to be fearful. If we dwell on the negative it can bring us down. Worry can worm its way into our thoughts and gnaw at our emotions. It has always been this way, of course. Every generation has faced reasons for trepidation. It was so even two thousand years ago, and it was why Jesus told his fear-wracked followers:

"Peace I leave with you; my peace I give you. I do not give to you as the world gives. Do not let your hearts be troubled and do not be afraid."[12] A short time later he added, *"I have told you these things, so that in me you may have peace. In this world you will have trouble. But take heart! I have overcome the world."*[13]

We experience personal peace when we are filled with the fruit of the Spirit, love. That fruit—produced in our lives by God alone—bears the blossoms of peace. It's not a sappy emotion but a robust confidence, a certainty anchored in the overcoming power of Christ. It doesn't mean that the troubles will go away. They won't. *"You will have trouble,"* Jesus said. But the difficulties and challenges we face will not rule us if the peace of Christ is ruling in our hearts. His power trumps all other powers.

I remembered this truth when I sat on a pile of rocks in the most unlikely place, a village in southern Sudan. I was there as a participant in a humanitarian mission to people displaced by years of brutal warfare. We conversed with a pastor who told us of the trials he had endured—the loss of his son, the burning of his village, horrendous destruction including multiple bombings that reduced his church to rubble. After ten years as a refugee he had returned to establish a new church in the very place where he had suffered such heartache and loss. We asked what made him want to come back. He answered firmly: "I came back to show the love of Christ and to proclaim him as the Prince of Peace." As I think back to that amazing moment I see his radiant face and realize anew that a love-driven life is truly a life ruled by peace.

A Life Calmed by Patience

With many people (possibly someone you know?) one of the toughest times to be love-driven is when driving. It's as if something happens to the psyche as soon as the ignition key is turned. Some individuals become a different person when they get behind the wheel—profoundly impatient, especially with other drivers who aren't as focused and intelligent! I'm guilty of this from time to time; but I remember to my shame that it's impossible to be simultaneously loving and impatient. If I am truly to be love-driven, I must practice patience in every relationship and every activity—even when driving!

Patience packs a lot of power. It can defuse potentially explosive moments. It can communicate understanding to someone who feels hopelessly misunderstood. It can transcend offensive acts or abusive words. The power to be patient comes from God's strength, not our own. As Paul explained to the Colossians, *Being strengthened with all power according to his glorious might so that you may have great endurance and patience.*[14] It is a spiritual fuel that keeps us going and enables us to endure everything that life throws at us.

As we live in obedience to Christ, as we are filled with the Spirit and bear the fruit of love, we can do anything and everything. Paul exclaimed: *I can do all things through Christ who strengthens me!*[15] As I wrap my mind around that thought I realize just how silly it is to be impatient. And I realize as well just how patient God is with me. He puts up with so much! That was Paul's testimony, too. In fact, he considered himself the worst of all sinners; but his sinfulness was completely enveloped by God's grace. He wrote: *But for that very reason I was shown mercy so that in me, the worst of sinners, Christ Jesus might display his immense patience as an example for those who would believe in him and receive eternal life.*[16]

Patience is a priority in the little things of life as well as the big. Whether putting up with traffic or putting up with an offensive person...whether dealing with an unruly child or dealing with a potentially life-altering situation...whatever we face must be faced with patience. In confronting the big things—the formidable challenges—we are wise to remember this advice from James: *Be patient, then, brothers, until the Lord's coming. See how the farmer waits for the land to yield its valuable crop and how patient he is for the autumn and spring rains. You too, be patient and stand firm, because the Lord's coming is near. Don't grumble against each other, brothers, or you will be judged. The Judge is standing at the door!*[17] Then James concludes: *Brothers, as an example of patience in the face of suffering, take the prophets who spoke in the name of the Lord. As you know, we consider blessed those who have persevered. You have heard of Job's perseverance and have seen what the Lord finally brought about. The Lord is full of compassion and mercy.*[18]

Love-driven patience deals with the present by remembering the past and looking to the future. It sees in the past the inspiring examples of believers who patiently endured almost unimaginable difficulties. It sees in the future the promise of ultimate redemption and reward.

The Lord is being patient, too—patient in offering us his salvation before he comes again. The Apostle Peter cautioned:

The Lord is not slow in keeping his promise, as some understand slowness. He is patient with you, not wanting anyone to perish, but everyone to come to repentance. But the day of the Lord will come like a thief. The heavens will disappear with a roar; the elements will be destroyed by fire, and the earth and everything in it will be laid bare. Since everything will be destroyed in this way, what kind of people ought you to be? You ought to live holy and godly lives as you look forward to the day of God and speed its coming. That day will bring about the destruction of the heavens by fire, and the elements will melt in the heat. But in keeping with his promise we are looking forward to a new heaven and a new earth, the home of righteousness. So then, dear friends, since you are looking forward to this, make every effort to be found spotless, blameless and at peace with him. Bear in mind that our Lord's patience means salvation.[19]

What a compelling statement! We can draw great encouragement from the fact that God is patient with us, that he doesn't want anyone to perish, that he wants every person to come to repentance. Peter's question is deeply convicting: *What kind of people ought you to be?* With eternity in view, how can we not be driven by love for the Lord whose patience means our very salvation?

A Life Guided by Kindness

Kindness is goodness in action. It is the heart and mind in work clothes—practical and effective. When I think of kindness, certain individuals come to mind—people who freely and readily say gracious words, do considerate deeds, react with courteous attitudes. Their Christlike demeanor inspires me to be kind—especially when I'm tempted to be just the opposite. Many of these kind souls have walked a rough road through life. Hugo Lopez is such a person.

I first saw Hugo making his way down a dirt path through a place called Pavas. About a dozen very noisy children swarmed him. An enormous smile beamed from his round face as he tossed brightly colored pieces of candy to the kids, stopping from time to time to hug and be hugged. A young man who was accompanying us into Pavas said, "They call him 'Hugo the Hugger'." We were instantly intrigued.

Hugo is the unofficial chaplain of Pavas, an impoverished "community" on the outskirts of San José, the capital city of Costa Rica. Pavas, in fact, is the largest slum in Central America. It teems with nearly 100,000 people—the majority of them single mothers and children. They live in shacks of cardboard and salvaged sheet metal, without indoor plumbing and for the most part without electricity—the only exceptions being those who have dared to tap into nearby power lines. Pavas reeks; but the literal stench of poverty is exceeded by the moral stench of human trafficking. Girls as young as 11 are sold by the pimps of Pavas day after day, night after night. For most of them, there is no way out; indeed, their very mothers were likely prostitutes themselves. It is a vicious, cruel cycle of existence.

Hugo was born into this world. His father was a raging drunk who raped Hugo's mother when she was only 14 years old. She gave birth to Hugo, then to one child after another. After the fifth child, profound depression drove her to take her own life. Hugo's father—who had never been anything but his biological father—died in a ditch from causes unknown. Hugo was left to fend for himself. He subsisted on anything he could scavenge, even garbage. A severe stutter made him even more self-conscious than he had already become. Hugo was homeless and hopeless. But one day he met a young couple who were for some reason drawn to him. They both gave Hugo something he had never received—a hug. "I was overwhelmed with their kindness," he told us. "I had never felt love like that. And then they told me about the greatest love of all...the love of Jesus, who sacrificed his life for my salvation. I believed in Jesus and I received his salvation; and I decided that day that I would give to children in the slums the same things I wanted for all those years—a hug, an 'I love you', a smile, a kind word."

Our faces streaked with tears, we encircled Hugo that day and prayed with him. Then we joined him on a journey into the heart of Pavas, each of us carrying a large box of food. As Hugo led the way, children tagged along, drawn to him like a human magnet. We stopped at one shack after another, giving food, and—like Hugo—giving hugs. It was especially touching to see at least a moment of joy in the faces of single moms who live in the daily desperation of poverty. At one point, Hugo said, "The people here need food and clothing and lots of other things. But there's nothing more valuable we can give them than the loving kindness of Jesus."

I've been back to Pavas on many occasions, and God willing I'll keep going back. The needs there are overwhelming; but I've learned from Hugo's loving example that overwhelming kindness can conquer overwhelming needs. Kindness is one of the most beautiful qualities we can express as God's children. It reflects his very goodness in us. It draws a sharp contrast against the background of unkindness and ugliness in this world. It goes against the tide of self-absorbed behavior so prevalent in our culture.

There is no question that a life driven by love is a life guided by kindness, for kindness is at the very heart of God's eternal plan. Paul stated it so magnificently: *God raised us up with Christ and seated us with him in the heavenly realms in Christ Jesus, in order that in the coming ages he might show the incomparable riches of his grace, expressed in his kindness to us in Christ Jesus.*[20]

A Life Guarded by Goodness

Do you know any identical twins? If so, you have probably experienced the frustration of trying to tell them apart. Which is which? Who is who? I once thoroughly humiliated myself by greeting and hugging a woman at church I thought to be a well-known friend. It turned out that she was not my friend after all but her identical twin—someone I didn't even know existed! The mix-up was a good laugh for the sisters but a red-faced moment for me.

Some qualities—like some people—are hard to tell apart. Kindness and goodness, for example, are nearly identical twin virtues. They are very similar; but there is a distinction. Kindness is primarily outward while goodness is primarily inward. Kindness is seen in behavior; goodness is seen in character. Kind words, actions and reactions are outer expressions of the inner quality of God's goodness that lives in the heart.

In his letter to the Christians at Ephesus, Paul wrote: *For you were once darkness, but now you are light in the Lord. Live as children of light (for the fruit of the light consists in all goodness, righteousness and truth).*[21] Notice that final phrase: *the fruit of the light consists in all goodness, righteousness and truth.* Those three qualities—goodness, righteousness and truth—reside in the character of spiritually enlightened souls: the *children of light.* That character is then expressed through good, righteous and truthful living.

Goodness is not inherently present in us. We are not by nature good. Quite the opposite, in fact. The Prophet Jeremiah said pointedly: *The heart is deceitful above all things and beyond cure.*[22] Sounds hopeless, but the encouraging news is that God offers us a purified heart that seeks his will and his glory. King David of Israel is described in the Bible as *"a man after God's own heart."*[23] But David was deeply flawed and guilty of some heinous sins. However, God in his mercy redeemed and renewed David's heart, and God's goodness filled his life when David prayed, *"Create in me a clean heart, O God; and renew a right spirit within me."*[24] The goodness that is the Spirit's fruit counteracts all that is bad and detrimental to spiritual health. It is like the antibodies that fight off infection and disease in the physical body. It has a purifying, protective effect because it is God at work in us.

Just like David, we are flawed and prone to failure. And just like him we need to pray for a clean heart and a right spirit. God will answer; he will give his Spirit. And the primary fruit of that Spirit is love—love that drives us to desire what is good and righteous and true.

A final thought about love and goodness: Jesus told his followers: *"But I tell you who hear me: Love your enemies, do good to those who hate you...Do to others as you would have them do to you."*[25] This is a hard truth. It's easy to love those who love us, but love our enemies? Do good to those who hate us? Yes, but we can't do it in our own strength. Only by the power of the Spirit infusing our lives with goodness are we able to love everyone...even our enemies.

A Life Proven through Faithfulness

Faithfulness is spiritual dependability. In just about every one of Paul's epistles there is a clear statement about the priority of faithfulness. In the very first verse of Ephesians, he addresses *the saints in Ephesus, the faithful in Christ Jesus.*[26] At the outset of Colossians, he writes, *To the holy and faithful brothers in Christ at Colosse.*[27] To his spiritual son, Timothy, he repeatedly reinforced this same truth. And throughout the Bible we see that faithfulness is essential to serving God, to declaring his Word, to helping other believers and to handling situations of responsibility.

From the Old Testament straight through the New, the wise, effective servant is shown to be totally faithful. We see this virtue in Joseph when he was unjustly imprisoned. We observe it in Moses as he managed an entire nation in the middle of a wasteland. We find it in Daniel, who ran a government and could not be put down by his enemies, for *they could find no corruption in him, because he was trust-worthy.*[28] We see it in Epaphroditus, a beloved co-worker of the Apostle Paul whom he called a faithful worker, a faithful soldier and a faithful messenger.[29] So deep was his commitment that he almost died for the work of Christ, risking his life to make up for the help the Philippians were unable to give to Paul.

To be a faithful servant of Jesus, you must handle the small things with the same regard as the big things. Jesus said, *"Whoever can be trusted with very little can also be trusted with much, and whoever is dishonest with very little will also be dishonest with much. So if you have not been trustworthy in handling worldly wealth, who will trust you with true riches? And if you have not been trustworthy with someone else's property, who will give you property of your own?"*[30] The implication is clear: the greater your dependability, the greater your blessing.

Love-driven servants see that everything in life is sacred, everything is to be devoted to the Lord. Whatever your talents, whatever your treasures, all are to be dedicated to God. *...Whatever you do, do it all for the glory of God.*[31] And don't hoard the secret things of God; share them liberally. As followers of Jesus, we have access to what the Bible calls mysterious truth; but we're also given permission to share the secret. Tell it freely and eagerly, for no area of loving, faithful dependability is more important than spreading the Good News.

A Life Strengthened by Gentleness

Nearly all modern English versions of the Bible refer to the next quality as *gentleness*.[32] The King James Version uses the word *meekness*. Both terms evoke similar thoughts of tenderness, weakness and mildness—a kind of wimpishness, really. But the original word has a very different connotation: it means *strength under control*. The ancient Greeks used the same root word to describe the effect of the bit in a horse's mouth—an easy-to-understand image of strength brought under control. With a simple piece of metal, a great animal is calmed into a gentle state.

Gentleness is not a weak, submissive, please-run-over-me attitude; it's a love-driven determination to live in a decisive yet humble and non-judgmental way with others. A few short verses after he describes the fruit of the Spirit, Paul writes this: *If someone is caught in a sin, you who are spiritual should restore him gently. But watch yourself, or you also may be tempted. Carry each other's burdens, and in this way you will fulfill the law of Christ.*[33] It takes courage to do this; but if a fellow follower of Christ is overcome by sin of any kind, the loving response is to restore that person in a spirit of gentleness—remembering all the while that any one of us could falter and fail at any time. That's why we need to watch ourselves, to guard against temptation, and to carry each other's burdens. Gentleness lifts up the one who has fallen. Gentleness recognizes that human frailty is our default setting (no pun intended!).

There is great strength in gentleness. Think of three men described in Scripture as being gentle or meek: Jesus, Paul and Moses. All three endured trials and travails that few of us can even begin to comprehend. Yet they demonstrated "strength under control" even in the throes of suffering; and none of them were weak in any way. Think especially of Jesus, our Savior, whose gentleness was evident even as he hung dying on the cross. In the depth of that agony he turned to the thief being crucified alongside him and said with gentle love, *"Today you will be with me in paradise."*[34] Jesus—whose life was always driven by love—is our enduring example of gentleness. May we look to him and learn the lesson well.

A Life Governed by Self-control

"You are out of control!" The young woman's voice was so loud and so unexpected, it brought the entire restaurant to a state of paralyzed silence. Instinctively, my eyes did a panoramic sweep of the scene. Everyone appeared to be thinking the same thing: *I can't believe she just did that.* But I wasn't taken completely by surprise. Her table was in my direct line of sight and I had been watching the commotion for some time. I could tell that things were getting increasingly out of hand as the woman attempted to tame the most unruly of creatures: a toddler who had reached the point of maximum unmanageability. Her husband—at the table but on his cell phone the entire time—seemed oblivious to the misbehavior going on mere inches away. The child was talking back, throwing food, breaking crayons, kicking the table and getting louder and louder. Finally, something snapped and the young mom erupted like a verbal volcano. When she screamed, "You are out of control!" I could tell that she was instantly shaken by her own outburst. The expression on her reddened face seemed to say, *Maybe I'm out of control, too.* She struggled from her seat, swept the rowdy child into her arms and rushed toward the exit.

That toddler was out of control because he was insisting on being *in control*. He didn't want anyone telling him what to do or what not to do. Unfortunately, many adults are just like that little boy: they want to live without restrictions. For them, *self-control* means that *self-is-in-control*—calling the shots, making the rules, doing whatever brings personal pleasure. For the Christian, life simply cannot be lived this way. The fruit of the Spirit is manifested in self-control—which means *self-under-control*, not *self-in-control*. It is the core of Jesus' command to his disciples: *"If anyone would come after me, he must deny himself and take up his cross and follow me."*[35]

There are three commands in that simple statement: 1) deny self; 2) take up the cross; 3) follow Jesus. All three require a measure of self-control. To deny self means to say no to selfish desires, to reject self-centered inclinations. To take up the cross means to willingly sacrifice, to willingly give. To follow Jesus means to walk in his steps of obedience to the Father's will.

Self-control is not the product of human initiative or intentionality. It is super-human—because it can only be produced by the power of God's Spirit working in the human mind, emotions and will. Almighty God—the God of infinite Love—who was so driven by love that he gave his one and only Son for our salvation, is the very One who fills us with that love and enables us to desire his will above our own. But therein lies a mystery as well: He doesn't choose for us, but he does empower us to choose. To choose his way over our way. To choose to deny ourselves. To choose to take up our cross. To choose to follow him.

CHAPTER THREE

THE WAY

Love is the Way of the Believer

And now I will show you the most excellent way.

1 Corinthians 12:31

He is the best-selling author in history. No one else even comes close. More impressions of his writings have been reproduced than any other man who has ever lived. Billions upon billions of copies of his books have been printed and distributed—so many that no one really knows how many. According to the most recent count, his works have been translated into more than 1,400 languages worldwide. His track record in publishing will never be eclipsed.

Born into a prominent family and raised in a highly cultured environment, he had advantages that others only dreamed of. From childhood he excelled, spurred by his superb teachers but more so by his formidable intellect. He was without question a genius. Trained in the law, he began his career and rapidly gained a reputation for his extraordinary powers of argumentation. His brilliance was surpassed only by his zeal. In fact, by his own testimony, no one was more driven to succeed.

He was such a perfectionist that he considered himself faultless in holding to the highest moral code. But there were certain people who made him so angry that he admitted wanting to kill them! They were men and women whom he later described as *"followers of the Way"*[1]—a Way that he could not tolerate under any circumstances. He convinced some of the leading judicial authorities to actually grant him permission to arrest and punish the offenders who dared to follow what he considered to be subversive dogma. With warrants in hand he departed for a city where he knew the radicals to be holed up. He would make sure they got what was coming to them.

All of these things happened long before he ever penned his first book. In fact, what he was about to experience became a theme in his later writings. But first, back to the story…

En route to the city where he intended to accost the rebels, something completely otherworldly happened. As he neared his destination a burst of light brighter and more intense than he could have imagined possible flashed around him. The magnitude of the blast of light instantly blinded him. He fell to the ground and heard an unknown voice calling his name and asking, *"Why are you persecuting me?"*[2] Stunned and confused, he replied, *"Who are you?"*[3] The answer reverberated back to him: *"I am Jesus, whom you are persecuting. Now get up and go into the city, and you will be told what you must do."*[4]

His traveling companions stood speechless and motionless. They heard the sound but didn't see a soul. Helping their leader to his feet, they led him by the hand into the city. Locked in a sightless world, he remained utterly inert, not eating or drinking anything for three days. Alone with his thoughts he must have constantly replayed that astonishing moment when a voice called out his name, followed by a haunting question: *"Saul, Saul...why are you persecuting me?"*[5] And then to hear those stunning words: *"I am Jesus, whom you are persecuting."*[6] The implication was unmistakable: In persecuting these "followers of the Way" he had been persecuting Jesus himself!

"I am Jesus," the voice said. That would have been the last name the proud but now blind Saul expected to hear. Jesus! The very man who embodies "the Way". The very man who inspires such devotion from his followers. Saul perhaps wondered to himself... *I've been persecuting him! I*

thought I was bringing justice to religious lawbreakers, but in pursuing them I was persecuting him? What in the world have I done?

Across town from where Saul was staying lived a "follower of the Way" named Ananias. God spoke to him in a vision, calling out his name as he did with Saul. The voice said firmly, *"Ananias!"*[7] and the disciple answered, *"Yes, Lord."*[8] Then came an odd instruction: *"Go to the house of Judas on Straight Street and ask for a man from Tarsus named Saul, for he is praying. In a vision he has seen a man named Ananias come and place his hands on him to restore his sight."*[9] We aren't given the exact details, but apparently Saul had received divine instructions regarding Ananias. In his blinded state Saul was undoubtedly encouraged to hear that he would see again. It was good news indeed; but for Ananias the prospect was actually terrifying. Upon getting his marching orders he replied, *"Lord, I have heard many reports about this man and all the harm he has done to your saints in Jerusalem. And he has come here with authority from the chief priests to arrest all who call on your name."*[10]

Bad news travels fast and the word had gotten to Damascus that a frightening man named Saul was on the warpath against any and all who dared to follow Jesus. Understandably, Ananias was more than a bit unsettled by the assignment. It was as if he had just been told to go visit a deluded murderer. But God answered the objections categorically, saying to Ananias: *"Go! This man is my chosen instrument to carry my name before the Gentiles and their kings and before the people of Israel. I will show him how much he must suffer for my name."*[11]

This news must have sent Ananias's mind reeling. A greatly feared man, the infamous Saul of Tarsus, had been chosen by God to be in the vanguard of the very Way that he once reviled! He would be an envoy for God's kingdom, and in so doing he would himself suffer much for bearing the name of Jesus. Ananias obeyed the directive, going immediately to Straight Street and entering the house of a man named Judas. He went to the helpless Saul, placed his hands on him and pronounced, *"Brother Saul, the Lord—Jesus, who appeared to you on the road as you were coming here—has sent me so that you may see again and be filled with the Holy Spirit."*[12] Instantly, something like scales fell from Saul's eyes. He could see again! He got up and was baptized, and after eating some food he began to regain his strength. Saul—the newest "follower of the Way"—then spent several days with the disciples in Damascus.

Saul of Tarsus had experienced an amazingly dramatic conversion, transforming him from a hate-filled persecutor of Christians to one who would become a love-driven ambassador for Jesus. Nothing in his life would ever be the same. He had become, in words he would later write, *a new creation*.[13] Even his name would be changed. Saul, meaning *prayed for*, would become Paul, meaning *humble one*. The one who was prayed for by his enemies would be God's chosen, humble servant. His heart, once so cold toward those who believed in Jesus and accepted him as Messiah, was now warm with loving regard. The road ahead would be rough, filled with perils and pitfalls of all kinds. But Paul would make the journey and make all the sacrifices demanded of him. He would endure ridicule, abuse, threats, beatings, imprisonments, snakebites, shipwrecks and more. Through it all he would learn the deep meaning of "the Way" and would be unceasingly changed by it. He would discover that the way of the believer is the Way of Love.

Paul's writings, penned mostly during his times in prison, were initially letters to churches or groups of Christians in various places. In one of those letters, written to disciples in Corinth (the "sin city" of that era), Paul would capture in a few hundred words an encyclopedia's worth of content about the supremacy of love. It is the highest and best prose ever written on the subject. It is preceded by a lengthy passage describing the reality of spiritual gifts and the interworking of members within the body of Christ. Paul concludes that long section with a promising statement: *And now I will show you the most excellent way.*[14]

Notice the final word of that statement: *Way*. It is the same Greek word—*hodos*—that Jesus used to describe himself as *"the way and the truth and the life."*[15] It is also the same term Paul used to describe believers as *followers of the Way.*[16] Here, in the final phrase of 1 Corinthians 12, Paul again writes *hodos* to describe *the most excellent way*. And what is this way? It is the Way of Love.

God's chosen ambassador to the world, Paul the Apostle, was once a hate-driven man. He despised the followers of Christ. He sought to destroy them. But all that changed from the inside out. The new man—Paul the Humble One—was energized by a completely different power. In a subsequent letter to the Corinthians he wrote that *Christ's love compels us.*[17] In other words, it moves us on, it urges us forward. It *drives* us. We are to be—like God himself— driven by love.

Let's take in the beauty of Paul's description of this love....

> *If I speak in the tongues of men and of angels, but have not love, I am only a resounding gong or a clanging cymbal. If I have the gift of prophecy and can fathom all mysteries and all knowledge, and if I have a faith that can move mountains, but have not love, I am nothing. If I give all I possess to the poor and surrender my body to the flames, but have not love, I gain nothing.*
>
> *Love is patient, love is kind. It does not envy, it does not boast, it is not proud. It is not rude, it is not self-seeking, it is not easily angered, it keeps no record of wrongs. Love does not delight in evil but rejoices with the truth. It always protects, always trusts, always hopes, always perseveres.*
>
> *Love never fails. But where there are prophecies, they will cease; where there are tongues, they will*

be stilled; where there is knowledge, it will pass away. For we know in part and we prophesy in part, but when perfection comes, the imperfect disappears. When I was a child, I talked like a child, I thought like a child, I reasoned like a child. When I became a man, I put childish ways behind me. Now we see but a poor reflection as in a mirror; then we shall see face to face. Now I know in part; then I shall know fully, even as I am fully known.

And now these three remain: faith, hope and love. But the greatest of these is love.[18]

Immediately following these unforgettable verses, Paul admonishes:

Follow the way of love...[19]

Love is not just a better way; it is the highest and best way. To follow the way of love is to live out the remarkable qualities described in 1 Corinthians 13. One by one, let's think on these things....

Love — More Eloquent than Eloquence

If I speak in the tongues of men and of angels,
but have not love, I am only a resounding
gong or a clanging cymbal.[20]

To put it even more bluntly: I may be the greatest communicator in the world, able to speak with angelic ability and in multiple languages; but if I am not driven by love in my heart then I am just a big noise. I'm as irritating as the crash of a gong or the clang of a cymbal.

Without love, even the most eloquently delivered words are meaningless. The point is not that there's something inherently wrong with eloquence but that love must underlie our inter-personal communications. In fact, there is nothing more beautiful than eloquently expressed love. As human beings we relate to one another through speech; and especially as "followers of the Way" what we say must be undergirded with genuine Christlike affection. If it isn't, the most excellently phrased sentence is not only empty; it can also be damaging.

Some of the most superbly crafted passages in the works of Shakespeare are those in which one character verbally dissects another with a clever barrage of words. A friend gave me a mug decorated with an assortment of those insults. Among the ones suitable for quoting...

Thine face is not worth sunburning.

Thou art as a candle, the better burnt out.

Thy brain is as dry as the remainder biscuit after voyage.

Thou art as fat as butter.

Reading those words from time to time I can smile at the assaults only because they have no personal connection to me; but then I'm reminded that we can so easily use words to tear apart another human being, often before we realize we're doing it. Love keeps us from going that far. Love drives us to tame our tongues, to control our words and not be controlled by them.

Love — More Brilliant than Brilliance

If I have the gift of prophecy and can fathom
all mysteries and all knowledge...
but have not love, I am nothing.[21]

Imagine being able to look into the future and see the unseen. Imagine being capable of unraveling the mysteries of the universe. Imagine being the smartest person on the planet. What a heady thought—literally! Someone with such abilities would be infinitely influential and extraordinarily rich. Yet to possess all that knowledge and be without love would be completely, utterly empty. More brilliant than brilliance is the power of love—a power that illuminates life's path like nothing else.

In Paul's day, many Christians—especially those in Corinth—were absorbed by a desire for prophetic ability. They longed for special wisdom, and even became competitive about who within their circles was the best and brightest in discerning spiritual truths! They justified their behavior by claiming that they were concerned with godly gifts; but the Apostle told them that in comparing themselves with one another they were just being foolish.[22] He said, in essence, spiritual gifts are good and meaningful but there is something even better. There's a better way: The Way of Love.

Love — More Formidable than Faith

If I have a faith that can move mountains,
but have not love, I am nothing.[23]

Some members of Christ's body are blessed with the gift

of faith—an exceptional God-given capacity to believe the miraculous, to envision the impossible. They are able to trust in God's supernatural power to bring about unimaginable results. They are able to rely on him to provide and deliver in the most desperate situations. This is a marvelous spiritual ability; but, absent love, it has no significance. Without love, faith that could literally move a mountain is nothing.

Let's be careful not to misinterpret here. Faith is a good thing, a God-given thing. But love is a better thing; the best thing, in fact. And faith is incomplete unless it is coupled with love. It is for this reason that Paul concludes his magnificent tribute with this statement: *And now these three remain: faith, hope and love. But the greatest of these is love.*[24]

Love — More Superior than Sacrifice

If I give all I possess to the poor and surrender my body to the flames, but have not love, I gain nothing.[25]

I have spent most of my life in the relative comfort of America. In all the towns where I have lived and worked there have been pockets of poverty—neighborhoods where people have less, particularly in socio-economic terms. Without exception, these areas have been dingier, dirtier and more crime-ridden. Yet these blighted places actually look livable in comparison with others I have seen outside the U.S.

In Kibera, Kenya, I participated in a relief project among the poorest of the poor, in a "neighborhood" so foul that it simply cannot be adequately described. I believe it must be experienced (though I wouldn't necessarily recommend it). When I later watched a documentary about that very slum it brought back the overpowering *smells* of that wretched place. In the mire of those muddy paths (they couldn't be called streets) I comprehended in a new way the term *abject poverty*. I wanted to rescue people from that horrid place. I wanted to give all the cash in my pockets to help as many as possible. But what if I literally gave everything I own to help those poor souls? What if I surrendered myself to be completely consumed in such a noble cause? Would it matter? The answer, according to the Apostle Paul, is that it all depends. It all depends on love.

Why we do what we do is what truly matters. What drives us makes all the difference; and if we are not driven by love then it is all for naught. Extreme sacrifice to help the helpless and complete surrender to an ideal only mean something if the motivating power is love.

In the first three verses of 1 Corinthians 13 Paul draws four contrasts, showing love to be more eloquent than eloquence, more brilliant than brilliance, more formidable than faith and more superior than sacrifice. Next, he delves into definitions. Beginning at verse 4, he tells us what love looks like, both positively and negatively. We learn what the Way of Love is and what it is not.

A Way of Patience

Love is patient [26]

Why would patience be listed as the first definitive quality of love? Could it be because we are constantly confronted with the temptation to be impatient with others? We can put up with ourselves, but we're not so adept at putting up with others. In friendships, in marriage, in connections with co-workers and classmates, and in other relationships of life we are faced with a never-ending stream of challenges to our patience. Certain words or expressions or gestures irritate us. We get offended even when no offense is intended and then we're prompted to think unkind thoughts. Sometimes the unkind thought bursts forth in an unkind word or a sarcastic comment (often followed by an "I-was-just-kidding" excuse). There's a good reason that patience tops the list, and we don't have to think very hard as to why.

Love, however, is patient. This verse in the venerable King James Version says that love *"suffereth long"*. It holds out for a long time, even in the face of difficulty. It does not lose heart but patiently and even bravely endures misfortunes and troubles. It bears the offenses and even the injuries of others. According to Scripture, to be patient is to be *slow to become angry.*[27] Our natural tendency is to be quick to anger, but love holds that in check. Love remains patient. Love says to us internally: hold your temper...keep your calm...put up with the irritation...endure the difficulty...be like Jesus who showed perfect patience.

A Way of Kindness

Love is kind [28]

Around my town I've spotted a number of cars sporting bumper stickers that read: *Practice random kindness and senseless acts of beauty.* The first time I saw one of those I wondered where the phrase originated, so I looked it up online and discovered that it was purportedly first written on a placemat at a restaurant in Northern California in 1982. The author, a magazine editor, says that she intended it to encourage good behavior. It sounds admirable but it made me wonder, what would Paul say about this little motto? In light of 1 Corinthians 13, I believe that he would say that there ought to be nothing random about kindness, and that there's certainly nothing senseless in beautiful expressions of Christian charity. True kindness—driven by the love of Christ in our hearts—is intentional, not accidental. True kindness sees the meaning beyond the act, a meaning that was perfectly embodied in the character of Jesus.

In life we're often tempted to show kindness because we want to get something in return. This is never a good motive. As "followers of the Way" we express kindness because we are the recipients of kindness—the love-driven kindness that caused God to give his very own Son for our sake.

A Way without Envy

Love...does not envy [29]

The color of envy, as we all know, is green. But why? Why do we say that someone is "green with envy"? It actually goes back to antiquity, to a phrase that originated with the Greek description of a jealous person. They were said to be green-faced because of an overproduction of bile and a resulting greenish complexion. The Greek word translated "envy" in 1 Corinthians 13:4 is *zeloo*, meaning to *boil with emotion*. This word can be used in a good sense to describe the zealous pursuit of good. But it has a more prominent negative sense, meaning to *boil with jealousy*. That's the meaning in Paul's description: *Love does not envy*. It doesn't boil angrily at the thought of another person who has more material wealth, who is more attractive, or who is more successful. True love looks at such a person without resentment or unhealthy desire.

In a culture bent on amassing possessions and obsessed with physical beauty, it can be tough at times to resist "turning green". If we attempt to rely on our own power, resistance is futile. But if we plug into the power of real love not only can we resist, we can rejoice—giving thanks for what we have rather than feeling morose for what we don't have. Love produces in us a genuine gratitude and the ability to celebrates others' successes.

A Way without Boasting

Love...does not boast [30]

Boasting is one of the ugliest of human tendencies. Think back to your experiences in childhood and adolescence. Remember the braggarts? Remember those schoolmates who couldn't stop telling you about their latest acquisition, their most recent accomplishment, their superior ability? Remember the jocks who could recite every detail of their exploits on the field or on the court? Of course you remember them; and perhaps you recall, painfully, that you were one of them. The truth is, all of us have a bit of the braggart in us. We paint ourselves in the best possible light. We talk about what we just bought, where we just went, what we just did, who we just saw. We're all tempted to lapse into self-focused, self-congratulatory, self-aggrandizing talk that subtly (or maybe not-too-subtly) communicates "I'm better...I'm smarter...I'm more affluent...I'm moving up the ladder...."

Is this ever acceptable for a "follower of the Way"? Nope. Love keeps its mouth shut about itself. Love draws no attention to itself. Love chooses to commend others and to resist commending one's own abilities, accomplishments and acquisitions. *Love does not boast.*

A Way without Pride

Love...is not proud [31]

Remember the near-identical twin virtues of kindness and goodness? They have a negative counterpart: the evil twins of pride and boasting. These vices differ in that pride is primarily internal and boasting is external. Pride stays inside and says, "Wow, am I ever great!" Boasting goes out and actually proclaims it. It is possible to be very prideful without ever openly boasting. In fact, between these ugly twins, pride may be the harder to deal with because it is so hidden; it is the root sin. Pride in the heart leads to boasting with the mouth. The biblical word for pride means "inflated"—literally, puffed up into an abnormal size. Think of all those cartoons in which the excessively proud man puffs out his chest so far that his buttons pop right off his shirt. Pride causes us to inflate who we really are and to think of ourselves more highly than we ought to think.

Love, however, is the antithesis of pride. It is the diametric opposite. It is the attitude that caused John the Baptist to say of Jesus, *"He must increase and I must decrease."* [32] There is no way to be simultaneously full of love and full of pride; the two cannot co-exist. So many relationships begin to disintegrate when one or both individuals develop proud, stubborn positions about any variety of things. It could start out with an unbending opinion on something minor and unimportant, then grow as increasingly larger things are added until so much negativity has piled up that a seemingly impassable blockage results. To dismantle the blockage in a relationship it is almost always necessary to first see prideful positions and opinions and declarations for what they are. Love is willing to do that because *love is not proud*.

A Way without Rudeness

Love...is not rude [33]

My mother used to tell me, "Crudeness is rudeness, and don't you dare be either crude or rude." She drilled it into my young mind that vulgar behavior is simply unacceptable. I understood that to include tasteless speech, bathroom humor, questionable slang, cursing of any kind, insults and sharp responses (especially to my elders). And because it came from my mother I processed this as basic law. It was only much later that I learned it to be basic love—an expression of Christ-like, God-honoring character. As a believer in Jesus and a "follower of the Way" I discovered that Mom was exactly on-point when she equated crudeness with rudeness. The descriptive term in the simple statement *love is not rude* covers both.

Sadly, our world is becoming ruder and cruder by the minute. Conversational speech even at the elementary school level is peppered with expletives. Innuendo used to be sprinkled throughout television programs; today, characters just come right out with outrageous statements about what they're thinking or feeling—and the viewers start replicating that very behavior. It is increasingly difficult to stand as a Christian against this tide of smuttiness in our culture. Only the power of love can enable us to do so successfully. Love resists unwholesome speech. Love stifles the verbal comeback we so want to deliver in response to an offense. Love does what is gentle and kind, for *love is not rude.*

A Way without Selfishness

Love...is not self-seeking [34]

Magazines are a dying breed. Hundreds have gone out of business in recent years, victims of easier-to-access and cheaper online content. But among those that are still going strong is a monthly with the perfect name for the Me generation—*Self* magazine. With over five million avid readers,

Self succeeds by focusing on what is most important to most people—themselves. I'm sure that *Self* includes a lot of articles of genuine benefit; my point is really more about people in general than the magazine in particular. Our basic wiring as human beings is self-centered. We love to look in the mirror. We are hyper-aware of who we are, what we want, what we need. In viewing a group photo we look first for our own image among the faces. The default setting in human nature is to love ourselves, first and foremost. But this presents a challenge to "followers of the Way".

Jesus said to his disciples, *"If anyone would come after me, he must deny himself and take up his cross and follow me. For whoever wants to save his life will lose it, but whoever loses his life for me will find it."*[35] There's an exquisite irony in Jesus' statement, a paradox that gives us a glimpse into how things work in the spiritual realm. If you want to save your life, Jesus says, you have to lose it. But if you do lose your life in following him, you will find it. This draws an absolute contrast and leads us to an absolute conclusion: if you truly love your life, you will totally love Jesus by giving him your life. The stark fact is that a self-seeking person ultimately loses while a Christ-seeking person ultimately wins. One of the beautiful qualities of love in a follower of Jesus is an absence of self-elevation, self-promotion or self-reliance. *Love is not self-seeking.*

A Way without Anger

Love...is not easily angered [36]

There are so many phrases to describe anger. I've heard or read several just in the past few days...

> *He flew off the handle...*
>
> *Her blood boiled...*
>
> *It was the latest incident of road rage...*
>
> *Venom spewed from his lips...*
>
> *She contorted her face in disgust...*
>
> *The teen's temper led to violence...*

Without much effort you could come up with a list of comparable phrases from your own conversations and your own reading. And why is this? Because anger is so prevalent in our society. Disturbingly prevalent. Of course, there are times when anger is appropriate and reasonable—when a loved one is threatened, for example. But in most situations of life, anger is inappropriate and unreasonable.

Certain individuals, unfortunately, have an extreme propensity for getting angry. Even the slightest, most insignificant thing can set them off like a Roman candle. Perhaps a particular person came to mind in the time it took you to read that sentence. I had a close relative who was quick-tempered. He was, most of the time, a wonderful Christian man. But the instant that something angered him, he was a different person—a person none of us wanted to be around. Later in life I think he finally learned that a love-driven follower of Christ is not easily angered. He mellowed; he became more reflective; he started filtering his words through the matrix of Christian love. Although he never said so, I'm sure that he regretted deeply those years that were so often punctuated with bursts of anger. Every one of those moments caused an imbalance in his life and in the lives of those closest to him. If he were here today I think he would say, learn it early and learn it well: *Love is not easily angered.*

A Way without Record Keeping

Love...keeps no record of wrongs.[37]

The car radio was tuned to a popular talk show famous for the host's expertise in dispensing advice on personal relationships. I was only half-listening when I heard a male caller say something that immediately caught my attention. "When my wife and I have a disagreement," he said, "she gets totally historical." The host interrupted him, chiming in, "Do you mean hysterical?" The man quickly replied, "No, I meant historical. She brings up everything that I ever did wrong over the history of our marriage!" I laughed, but then I realized how prone we are to remember what people have done to us and how incapable we seem in recalling our own faults and failings. As love-driven followers of Jesus we can't allow ourselves to fall into this pattern. Love, says 1 Corinthians 13:5, *keeps no record of wrongs.* It doesn't maintain a mental notebook filled with details of what others have done against us. Genuine, Christlike love not only forgives; it also forgets. Nothing gets filed away. Love shreds the evidence.

A Way without Enjoyment of Evil

Love does not delight in evil
but rejoices with the truth.[38]

In recent years a number of very prominent Christian leaders have fallen from their high positions of leadership. Many have shipwrecked their lives on the rocks of infidelity.

Some have been caught in shady financial dealings. Others have been snared in the net of greed. A few have actually been arrested and imprisoned for fraud, abuse, sexual misconduct, pornography and more. These are hideous and shameful things; and these sins take an immeasurable toll, much like a tsunami can claim more lives than the earthquake from which it was generated. But also hideous and shameful is the response of professed Christians who react with uncharitable attitudes, actually finding pleasure and satisfaction in the spectacular tumble of a once-esteemed leader. This merely adds sin to sin. Scripture is clear: *Love does not delight in evil but rejoices with the truth.*

It should give us no pleasure to hear that another person—especially a fellow believer—has failed. This applies not just to our attitude toward leaders whom we may not know and with whom we may not agree; it applies to our own relationships. Love never delights in the failings and faults of another person. *Love rejoices with the truth*—the truth that God's grace can triumph over everything that can possibly go wrong with us as sin-prone human beings.

A Way of Permanence

[Love] always protects, always trusts,
always hopes, always perseveres.[39]

Always is such a big word. It is explicit and unconditional. It leaves no doubt, no hint of maybe. *Always* means *always* —at all times, in all circumstances. Love—the love of Christ in the hearts of those who follow him—is for always. His love is not temporal; it is eternal and enduring. And it is this very love that infuses our lives.

Love always protects. In old English the word *protects* is sometimes translated *covereth.* In this term is the beautiful imagery of covering something of value in order to guard and preserve it. We see this same picture in the words of the Apostle Peter: *Above all, love each other deeply, because love covers over a multitude of sins.*[40] Love enables us to protect one another with a blanket of concern. Think of Red Cross workers wrapping warm blankets around disaster victims. What they give in physical aid can be likened to what we can give in spiritual aid to anyone in need.

Love always trusts. In human relationships, nothing is more important than trust. When there is doubt; when there is a hesitancy to believe the best; the relationship is on shaky ground. This is true as well of our relationship with God. Our trust in him is built on the bedrock of love. Paul wrote to the believers in Galatia about this connection between faith and love: *The only thing that counts is faith expressing itself through love.*[41] What a remarkable thought! The way that we live out our trust in Christ is through the day-in, day-out expression of love. Paul says it's the only thing that counts. Why? Because the life of love is all-inclusive. It encompasses every dimension of the human experience and the full scope of human relationships. Nothing is outside the bounds of faith expressing itself through love.

Love always hopes. In common usage, *hope* usually has a very different connotation from the biblical meaning. For example, when we say that we hope that a certain thing will happen there's always the possibility that it won't. There's an element of doubt, a prospect of disappointment. In the Scriptural sense, hope is a sure thing. It is definite. And that's because it is inextricably linked to the promise of salvation. We hope with confidence because of the object of our hope, Jesus himself. This is why Paul wrote in another epistle, *Hope does not disappoint us, because God has poured out his love into our hearts by the Holy Spirit, whom he has given us.*[42] Love empowers us to think and feel and act with eternity in view because love always hopes.

Love always perseveres. Love hangs on. It doesn't run away. It doesn't get frightened off by trials and misfortunes. The word *perseveres* means *endures.* Love endures—bravely, calmly, faithfully—no matter what happens. In his second letter to Timothy, Paul wrote: *Here is a trustworthy saying: If we died with him* [with Jesus], *we will also live with him; if we endure, we will also reign with him.*[43] Take note of that statement: *...if we endure, we will also reign with him.* The power to endure—to persevere—comes from the love of God at work in us. It will have a triumphant end.

A Way that Never Fails

Love never fails.[44]

The love of Christ within us is an unfailing love. In our relationships with others our love often falters and fails. We do things that we regret; we say things we wish we could take back. We have to apologize, retract and do our best to rebuild whatever we've broken. But Jesus loves us in an unfailing way; and as we are willing, he empowers us to love with his love. We won't achieve a state of perfection until we are actually with him, in his eternal presence. But we can grow in love, and we can be constantly encouraged that even when we mess up, he never lets us down. *Love never fails.*

A Way that Transcends All Other Ways

But where there are prophecies, they will cease; where there are tongues, they will be stilled; where there is knowledge, it will pass away. For we know in part and we prophesy in part, but when perfection comes, the imperfect disappears. When I was a child, I talked like a child, I thought like a child, I reasoned like a child. When I became a man, I put childish ways behind me. Now we see but a poor reflection as in a mirror; then we shall see face to face. Now I know in part; then I shall know fully, even as I am fully known. And now these three remain: faith, hope and love. But the greatest of these is love.[45]

God has chosen a variety of ways in which to reveal himself—through direct prophecies, through specific languages, through special knowledge. All of these will reach an end.

Prophecies will cease. Tongues will be stilled. Knowledge will pass away. But love will endure, and one day all who have put their trust wholly in Jesus will see Love face to face. Paul says it so poetically: *Now we see but a poor reflection as in a mirror; then we shall see face to face. Now I know in part; then I shall know fully, even as I am fully known.* This present, earthly life is full of riddles and enigmas that will never be solved until we are with our Lord. He knows us fully, better than we know ourselves; and one day we shall know even as we are known.

Faith, hope and love remain. But the greatest of these is love. The reason is clear: love is greater than faith because faith will be replaced with sight, and what we will see is love personified and perfect. We shall see him and be like him. This is the fulfillment of faith. Love is greater than hope because hope will come to fruition with the revelation of the one in whom we hope. Faith and hope are essential; but love is the sustaining grace of both. When faith and hope have accomplished their part, love will still be there. All three are great and wonderful; but *the greatest of these is love.*

Paul's very next words bring us back to the practical reality: *Follow the way of love....* [46] The way of the believer is faith-based and hope-filled; but above all else it is love-driven. Our imperative is clear: *Follow the way of love.*

CHAPTER FOUR
THE TEST
LOVE IS THE TEST OF THE TRUE

We know and rely on the love God has for us. God is love.
Whoever lives in love lives in God, and God in him.
1 John 4:16

Frank was an impressive young man. Courteous, charming and brimming with confidence, he left more than one mother thinking, 'I hope my daughter marries someone like him'. Frank's résumé was remarkable for a man his age. He had been a doctor, a lawyer, an airline pilot and an agent for the U.S. government. And, astonishingly, he had done it all before he turned 21! No wonder his life inspired a major motion picture and a hit show on Broadway.

But Frank wasn't what he seemed to be. When others looked at him they saw a man of extraordinary accomplishment. When Frank looked in the mirror he saw a liar, a cheat and a thief. He was accomplished all right—as an impostor, a forger, a con artist and a master of evasion. He had been arrested twice, and both times escaped from police custody—once from a taxiing airliner and once from a U.S. federal penitentiary! But Frank knew that his fake life was about to collapse of its own weight. A fiercely determined FBI agent was on his trail. The charade was about to come to an end.

On the day that Frank was cornered, arrested and taken into custody by the FBI, he felt a strange sense of relief. He had lived for years in fear and in bondage to an odd artificiality. He found himself desperately longing for reality, for authenticity.

After several years in prison, he was given a unique chance at redemption. Government officials offered him a work-release opportunity: Get out of jail by helping us understand how you succeeded as a criminal. Frank Abagnale jumped at the chance, earning his freedom and becoming one of America's leading security consultants. His life inspired the feature film *Catch Me If You Can*, as well as the Broadway musical of the same name.

It's easy to look at Frank's life and think, 'I certainly have nothing in common with him!' But maybe that isn't the case. Maybe we are more alike than we would care to admit. The fact is, every human being is prone to deception—especially self-deception. How readily we can mislead ourselves into thinking we're better than we really are. And all of us in one way or another are prone to fear—fear of failure, fear of consequences, fear of catastrophe. On the positive side of the equation, all of us long for authenticity. We yearn for a life that is real. But how do we get there? How can we know what is true? How can we experience what is really real?

There's a short book near the end of the Bible that addresses these questions head-on. It is actually a letter that the Apostle John wrote to Christians toward the end of the first century. Although ancient, its content is as relevant to us today as it was to those first recipients ages ago. Its message is simple and straightforward. Beautifully woven throughout the letter's fabric are two golden threads identified by two key words: *Love* and *Know*. These words each appear more than 40 times in this brief epistle. They are the central terms John uses in developing an all-important theme: Love is the Test of the True.

You've undoubtedly heard, "the proof is in the pudding." But, technically, you've heard wrong. The original saying—dating all the way back to the 14th century—goes like this: "The proof of the pudding is in the eating." In other words, authenticity is proven through experience.

I once saw an amazing exhibition of food that looked perfectly delicious and enticing, but it was all fake—the work of a team of Chinese "culinary artists" who have mastered the craft of artificial food. And, yes, one of the items on display was a bowl of pudding! It seemed real; it looked yummy; but it was nothing but plastic. The "proof" of that pudding would have been uncomfortably revealed in the eating!

Spiritual Authenticity

So, what does this have to do with living a love-driven life? Simply this: Spiritual authenticity is proven through experience. Love is something we practice. Otherwise, it isn't really love at all. John makes this point time and time again in the first of his three open letters to believers. He stresses that love is the test of true spiritual life and the true presence of God in us and with us.

John writes, *We know that we have passed from death to life, because we love our brothers. Anyone who does not love remains in death.*[1] Love is the test of true spiritual transformation. When speaking of someone who has died we often say that they "passed"—meaning that they have passed from this life to the next. But John's point is that as believers we have already passed—we have already gone from death to life. We already have eternal life! And the evidence of this transformation is the love we express for God and for others. God's love in us drives us to love in return—to love him, to love people, and—conversely—to not love this world or anything in it.[2] Love is the language of the present-tense spiritual reality in which we live right here, right now.

The Definition of God

Love is the test of the true—the true essence of God himself. 1 John 4:16 says, *God is love. Whoever lives in love lives in God, and God in him.*[3] With three simple words totaling just nine letters in English, John says something remarkably significant: *God is love.* He personifies love. He energizes love. He *is* love.

At the heart of the universe is a God whose very being is called love. Not power, not judgment, not even glory or wisdom or strength. Love. And it is a love we cannot escape. We can do our best to push it away, deny it, refuse it. But it surrounds us as much as the air we breathe. Writing to the Christians at Rome, Paul expressed it this way: *In all these things* [the trials of life] *we are more than conquerors through him who loved us. For I am convinced that neither death nor life, neither angels nor demons, neither the present nor the future, nor any powers, neither height nor depth, nor anything else in all creation, will be able to separate us from the love of God that is in Christ Jesus our Lord.*[4] Yes, God is love. He is its very definition. And, as John states so clearly, if we live in love we live in God, and God in us.

A Reason for Confidence

Love at work in us gives true spiritual confidence. It enables us to face every day with certainty and to face the future without worry or dread. John writes, *In this way love is made complete among us so that we will have confidence on the day of judgment, because in this world we are like him. There is no fear in love. But perfect love drives out fear, because fear has to do with punishment. The one who fears is not made perfect in love.*[5]

History is headed to a climax. All of us—all humanity of all the ages—will one day stand before our Creator to be judged. What a sobering thought! Yet we can look to that day with confidence because of God's love present and perfected in us. Our confidence comes from being spiritually secure in our Lord. John explains that *in this world we are like him—*

meaning we who are followers of Jesus are like him. And being like him, we have no reason to fear.

There is no fear in love because if we are truly in God and he in us, what is there to fear? Not death, not judgment, not any of the potentially frightening things wrong in this present world, because though we are *in* this world we are not *of* this world.[6]

Loss, illness, poverty, loneliness—none of these should strike fear into the heart of any child of God. Why? Because fear, as John says, has to do with punishment; but held firm in the grip of love, we are safe from every reason to be apprehensive. The most-repeated command in all of Scripture is this: *Don't be afraid*. It is frequently stated: *Fear not*. This message was communicated by the prophets, by the apostles, by angels, and by Jesus himself. We don't have to be afraid because, as John explains, *the one who is in you* [Jesus] *is greater than the one who is in the world* [Satan and all his evil spirits].[7] When we live in love—anchored in God himself— we can be truly confident because we are truly secure.

A century ago, the best-selling book in America was a sentimental novel titled, *In His Steps*. Within a decade after its release, more than 30 million copies were purchased worldwide. It is unique in publishing history because the book is actually better known for its subtitle—the instantly recognizable question, *What would Jesus do?*

In His Steps, set in the fictional town of Raymond (somewhere in the eastern United States), describes what happens when a group of Christians—led by a righteously-determined minister—make a covenant to actually live like Jesus for one year. Regrettably, the author's primary goal was not to encourage loving obedience to Christ so much as it was to promote new and popular expressions of Christian activism. The characters in the novel enlist in the temperance movement, advance the cause of women's suffrage, campaign for labor rights, and promote Christian influence over the arts. Noble pursuits, but many have questioned whether these would actually be the things that Jesus would do.

Many years after *In His Steps* was first published there was a resurgent interest in the question, *What would Jesus do?* Millions of Americans wore wristbands and sported apparel with the WWJD moniker. It was well intentioned; but it spawned innumerable pop-culture, half-mocking spin-offs—*What would so-and-so do?* Simply fill in the blank with your favorite choice.

A Better Question

In a previous chapter I mentioned the more definitive question that M. A. Thomas would ask repeatedly throughout the day: *How would Jesus love this person?* That was his matrix. Now let me suggest a third possibility:

What does love drive me to do, say or think?

I have found that this question has a powerful capacity to filter out the ineffective, hurtful and even detrimental things that I'm often tempted to do, say or think. This question works because it puts the mind of Christ and the character of God himself in the driver's seat of my actions, my words and my thoughts. He enables; I obey. It is the power of his love at work in my life.

I admit, sometimes I simply don't know what to do, say or think in a particular situation. But I often discover that uncertainty in such moments is a signal to wait on God and trust that he will keep his promise to give wisdom (and to give it generously).[8] I have also learned that there are many, many times in life when the loving thing is to keep my mouth shut, to stay still, to calm my mind.

Love is the test of the true—God's true reality, God's

true presence in us, God's true power lived out through us. Love is both the essence and the expression. When we express love, we are sharing Christ with others, bringing him who is love into whatever situation we face. John says very clearly that the person who claims to live in Jesus must walk in Jesus. That means to walk in the way of love. It's a way of sacrifice and service—not merely with words ...*but with actions and in truth*.[9] This, John explains, *is how we know that we belong to the truth.*[10]

Do you belong to the truth? Does your life pass the test of the true? Are you driven by love?

Let me repeat the question that I believe we should be asking continually:

What does love drive me to do, say or think?

A life driven by love will be defined by actions, words and thoughts that reflect the truth. That is what John's own life and experience show us.

A Life Transformed by Love

On the day that Jesus met John and his brother James he gave them a nickname: *Boanerges*—an Aramaic word that is best translated *Sons of Thunder*.[11] One biblical scholar explains that it means "the soon-angry ones." John and James were impetuous and quick-tempered. They were not known for their loving dispositions; quite the opposite. Luke's gospel describes an occasion in which the people of a particular Samaritan village did not properly welcome Jesus. John and James were so incensed that they asked, *"Lord, do you want us to call fire down from heaven to destroy them?"*[12] Jesus rebuked them, of course; but the incident revealed their true nature. In time, however, Christ spiritually transformed these two fiery brothers into very different men. James became the first martyred Apostle, put to death by Herod.[13] John became "the Apostle of Love" and throughout his gospel he refers to himself not by name but as *"the disciple whom Jesus loved."*[14] The dominant theme of his writings is the all-encompassing love of God. He had been changed by God's love and his life was then driven by it.

What about your life? What's driving you? What is the motivating power behind your actions, words and thoughts? Is it the presence of Jesus himself within you? If it is, you can ask with certainty, *What does love drive me to do, say or think?* God by his Spirit will then guide you. You can be sure that he will never direct you to do something against his revealed will, counter to his Word or in conflict with his Church.

Think back over the things we've seen in Love as the Mark of the Christian, Love as the Fruit of the Spirit and Love as the Way of the Believer. Did you notice the emphasis Scripture places on practical instructions, not abstract theories, in talking about love?

Remember the example of the Good Samaritan? He didn't offer a sermon; he acted out the truth. He saw someone in desperate need, felt that person's pain, took the risk, gave all that he was able to give, and promised to give even more. At every point, he did, said and thought the loving thing.

Remember Paul's epic treatise on love in 1 Corinthians 13? It isn't an ivory-tower composition; it is a practical description of life as it is meant to be lived—with relentless love that seeks what is highest and best.

Remember the beauty of love revealed in the fruit of the Spirit? It is love filled with joy, ruled by peace, calmed by patience, guided by kindness, guarded by goodness, proven through faithfulness, strengthened by gentleness, and governed by self-control. Each quality is an answer to the question, *What does love drive me to do, say or think?*

It is the genuine response of a joyful attitude even in the midst of difficulty.

It is a peaceful word spoken into a turbulent situation.

It is a patient reaction to an offense.

It is an act of kindness toward someone who may offer nothing in return.

It is a good, gentle thought toward someone whose own manner is neither good nor gentle.

It is a decision to be faithful when the temptation to break a promise is strong.

It is controlling the urge to be angry, taming the tongue in the instant that a verbal comeback would win an argument but damage a relationship.

It is in all these ways and more that we reveal that we belong to Jesus, that his Spirit directs us, that his love drives us.

In *The Message*, Ephesians 5:1-2 says, *"Watch what God does, and then you do it, like children who learn proper behavior from their parents. Mostly what God does is love you. Keep company with him and learn a life of love. Observe how Christ loved us. His love was not cautious but extravagant. He didn't love in order to get something from us but to give everything of himself to us. Love like that."*[15]

Learn a life of love. We don't become loving on our own. We have a pattern, a teacher. We have to learn love. We have to practice it. We have to actually do, say and think the loving thing. We can look at the life of Jesus and absorb how he loved. There was nothing cautious in his love. He held nothing back. He showed a full, absolute commitment to love. He put everything on the line. There was no "pre-nup" in the relationship with his Bride, the Church. His love was extravagant—immeasurably above and beyond the ordinary. He was driven by amazing love, never in order to get anything from us but to give everything to us. We need to practice loving like that. Is it possible? Yes, because he makes it possible. You *can* live a love-driven life! Inspired by the love of God for you, guided by the example of Jesus before you, and energized by the Holy Spirit in you, you can experience the extraordinary life God intends for you—a love-driven life.

REFERENCES

INTRODUCTION

1. John 5:36-39
2. John 1:1-4
3. John 1:10-12
4. John 3:2
5. John 3:3
6. John 3:4-8
7. John 3:9
8. John 3:10-15
9. John 3:16

CHAPTER ONE

THE MARK

1. John 13:33
2. John 13:34-35
3. *The Church at the End of the 20th Century*, Appendix II, p. 133. Francis A. Schaeffer. IVP, 1970.
4. John 15:9-13
5. John 15:17
6. Matthew 22:34
7. Matthew 22:35-36
8. Matthew 22:37-40
9. Deuteronomy 6:4-5
10. Leviticus 19:18b
11. Matthew 22:40
12. John 15:9-10
13. John 15:11
14. Luke 10:25
15. Luke 10:26
16. Luke 10:27
17. Luke 10:28
18. Luke 10:29
19. Luke 10:30-35
20. Luke 10:36
21. Luke 10:37
22. Luke 10:37
23. See John 4:9
24. Romans 13:8
25. 1 John 3:17
26. John 15:13

CHAPTER TWO

THE FRUIT

1 Galatians 5:22-23a

2 Galatians 5:13-14

3 James 1:2-3

4 John 15:9-11

5 Hebrews 12:1-2, NASB

6 Philippians 2:7

7 Colossians 3:2

8 Colossians 3:12-13

9 Colossians 3:14

10 Colossians 3:15

11 Philippians 4:7

12 John 14:27

13 John 16:33

14 Colossians 1:11

15 Philippians 4:13

16 1 Timothy 1:16

17 James 5:7-9

18 James 5:10-11

19 2 Peter 3:9-15

20 Ephesians 2:6-7

21 Ephesians 5:8-9

22 Jeremiah 17:9

23 Acts 13:22

24 Psalm 51:10, KJV

25 Luke 6:27-31

26 Ephesians 1:1

27 Colossians 1:2

28 Daniel 6:4

29 See Philippians 2:25-30; 4:18

30 Luke 16:10-12

31 1 Corinthians 10:31

32 Galatians 5:23

33 Galatians 6:1-2

34 Luke 23:43

35 Matthew 16:24

CHAPTER THREE

THE WAY

1 See Acts 22:4, NLT

2 Acts 9:4

3 Acts 9:5

4 Acts 9:5-6

5 Acts 9:4

CHAPTER THREE

THE WAY [CONT.]

6 Acts 9:5

7 Acts 9:10

8 Acts 9:10

9 Acts 9:11-12

10 Acts 9:13-14

11 Acts 9:15-16

12 Acts 9:17

13 See 2 Corinthians 5:17

14 1 Corinthians 12:31

15 John 14:6

16 See Acts 22:4, NLT

17 2 Corinthians 5:14

18 1 Corinthians 13:1-13

19 1 Corinthians 14:1

20 1 Corinthians 13:1

21 1 Corinthians 13:2

22 See 2 Corinthians 10:12

23 1 Corinthians 13:2

24 1 Corinthians 13:35

25 1 Corinthians 13:3

26 1 Corinthians 13:4a

27 James 1:19

28 1 Corinthians 13:4b

29 1 Corinthians 13:4c

30 1 Corinthians 13:4d

31 1 Corinthians 13:4e

32 John 3:30

33 1 Corinthians 13:5a

34 1 Corinthians 13:5b

35 Matthew 16:24-25

36 1 Corinthians 13:5c

37 1 Corinthians 13:5d

38 1 Corinthians 13:6

39 1 Corinthians 13:7

40 1 Peter 4:8

41 Galatians 5:6

42 Romans 5:5

43 2 Timothy 2:11-12

44 1 Corinthians 13:8a

45 1 Corinthians 13:8b-13

46 1 Corinthians 14:1

CHAPTER FOUR

THE TEST

1 1 John 3:14

2 See 1 John 2:15

3 1 John 4:16

4 Romans 8:37-39

5 1 John 4:17-18

6 John 17:14-16

7 1 John 4:4

8 See James 1:5

9 1 John 3:18

10 1 John 3:19

11 Mark 3:17

12 Luke 9:54

13 See Acts 12:1-2

14 See John 13:23; 19:26; 20:2; 21:7,20

15 Ephesians 5:1-2, *The Message*

SPECIAL NOTES:

*In the story beginning on page 36, the man named Roberto is a real person but his name has been changed to protect his identity.

**In the story beginning on page 41, the account of M.A. Thomas rescuing the three children in the New Delhi train depot, Rajeev is a nickname for the oldest boy, not his real name. He has taken a new Christian name and now serves as a highly-respected pastor in India.

A. Christian

A. Christian is a pseudonym. Although I have chosen to remain anonymous I can assure you that all of the experiences described in *The Love-Driven Life* are true. I have lived these things, and the truths I have discovered have changed my life. I pray that they will transform yours as well.